GEEKTIONARY

From ANIME to ZETTABYTE,
An A to Z Guide to All Things Geek

GEEKTIONARY

**MORE THAN 1,000 WORDS TO UNDERSTAND GOOBS,
GAMERS, ORKDORKS, AND TECHNOFREAKS**

GREGORY BERGMAN AND JOSH LAMBERT

Avon, Massachusetts

Published by
Adams Media, a division of F+W Media, Inc.
57 Littlefield Street, Avon, MA 02322. U.S.A.
www.adamsmedia.com

ISBN 10: 1-4405-1114-4
ISBN 13: 978-1-4405-1114-1
eISBN 10: 1-4405-1188-8
eISBN 13: 978-1-4405-1188-2

Printed in the United States of America.

10 9 8 7 6 5 4 3 2 1

Library of Congress Cataloging-in-Publication Data
Bergman, Gregory
Geektionary / Gregory Bergman and Josh Lambert.
p. cm.
ISBN 978-1-4405-1114-1
1. American wit and humor—Dictionaries. 2. Geeks (Computer enthusiasts)
—Humor. 3. Science fiction fans—Humor. I. Lambert, Joshua N. II. Title.
PN6165.B46 2010
818'.607—dc22
2010038956

This book is available at quantity discounts for bulk purchases.
For information, please call 1-800-289-0963.

CONTENTS

Chapter 1

GEEKOLOGY

What is a geek? The word "geek" has a long colorful history. It originally referred to a crazy person. More recently, it denoted sideshow performers who would bite off the heads off live chickens—an act few self-respecting geeks today partake in.

It was not until the 1980s that "geek" became slang for a person who was an expert in scientific and technological pursuits but lacked basic social skills. Isolated and shunned by his or her peers, this geek was thought to find solace in science fiction, fantasy, and comic books—perhaps to an unhealthy degree.

And then it happened. The dot.com boom changed the nature of the economy in the 1990s. Leading this new computer revolution was not the savvy ad man or financial shark of times past. Instead, it was . . . the geek. As Alpha-geeks such as Bill Gates, Jeff Bezos, and Steve Jobs became household names, the term "geek" began to take on a more positive connotation. After all, the high school geek of the 1980s now drove a Ferrari and dated supermodels, while the star quarterback who had tormented him was now long unemployed and drove an old pick-up truck to his new school and last hope: ITT Tech.

Is a geek the same as a nerd? No. While a geek may be obsessed with certain esoteric topics, he or she can still have an active social life—though often only with other geeks. The stereotypical "nerd," however, is more awkward, less confident, and more socially inept than the geek. In other words, a nerd is a geek who can't get a date. Even a room full of geeks would be able to spot the nerd.

We have written this book with geeks and geek wannabes in mind. If you want to fit in among the geeks, it would behoove you to study these terms and concepts. As we enter the era of the geek, knowing how to navigate geekdom may be your best chance of survival.

May the geek be with you!

404 *(noun)*
Named after a standard HTTP error code, 404 has come to mean: 1. To misplace something. 2. Someone who is clueless. 3. An Internet error or missing page.
My mom's keys are always 404.

alpha geek *(noun)*
The geekiest one of the bunch, appearing to be superior.
Bill Gates is the ultimate ALPHA GEEK.

analog *(adjective)*
When a person is boring or one-note.
He was, like, cute and all, but he was just so, like, ANALOG. It totally turned me off.

animatronic *(adjective)*
Describes mechanical people or animals like those seen at Chuck E. Cheese and Disneyland. Used in films such as *Jurassic Park* to depict dinosaurs.
My last girlfriend was ANIMATRONIC.

ansatsuken *(noun)*
A Japanese assassination martial art that has the goal of killing someone.
I warn you, before you try to take my lunch money, I am highly trained in the art of ANSATSUKEN.

anthropomorphism *(noun)*
To give an animal or a nonliving thing human characteristics. Anthropomorphism can be seen in Disney movies where the rabbits sing and dance or on *South Park* with a talking piece of poo, Mr. Hankey.
To say, "The sea was angry that day, my friends," would be to ANTHROPOMORPHIZE the ocean.

Betamax *(noun)*
When the better technology loses in the market to an inferior technology. Named for the Betamax, which was introduced by Sony in 1975 and replaced two years later by JVC's VHS.
The 3DO was superior to the Sega Genesis and Super Nintendo but was so expensive it went out like BETAMAX.

GEEK FACT

The last Sony Betamax was produced in 2002. Interestingly, it was found hiding out in a remote cave in the jungles of Iwo Jima.

booth bunny *(noun)*
A hot girl at a comic convention paid to hang out at a booth and help sell products using her looks.
That BOOTH BUNNY totally wanted me, so I bought $100 worth of Pokemon cards just so she knows I care.

GEEK FACT

If you are going to pick up a booth bunny at a comic book convention, be clever and use comic-book-related come-on lines:
Examples:
• Faster than a speeding bullet, more powerful than a locomotive.
• Pow! Crash! Boom! that's what I do.
• Ever heard of the Fantastic Four? Well, want to meet the fantastic 8½?

canon *(noun)*
Official elements in a fictional universe. The *Star Wars* movies are canon. But *Star Wars* fan fiction is not canon and, therefore, not an element in the universe.
The appearance of Star Wars *characters in* Soulcalibur IV *is not CANON.*

Cheech Wizard *(proper noun)*
A character developed by the artist Vaughn Bode that first appeared in the late 1960s. This and other psychedelic Bode creations are seen in graffiti and street art. Vaughn Bode's art and *Cheech Wizard* inspired the style of Ralph Bakshi's animated film, *Wizards*.
Forget Chong, the CHEECH WIZARD is the bomb!

Club 33 *(proper noun)*
A members-only club in Disneyland. The waiting list for membership is sixteen years.
CLUB 33 and the Ink and Paint Club from Who Framed Roger Rabbit? *are two clubs that I want to check out. Minnie Mouse is hot.*

comic sans *(noun)*
One of the most hated fonts in existence, so much so that there is a "ban comic sans" movement.
Typing an angry note to someone is made even more offensive if done in COMIC SANS.

continuity *(noun)*
The consistency of characters, plotlines, or details within a story.
Geeks love pointing out CONTINUITY errors.

cool hunter *(noun)*
An occupation involving the observation of cultural trends and prediction for the future of what is aesthetically cool.
Hey, COOL HUNTER, when is the 1970s platform shoe going to come back? Short guys are waiting on it!

GEEK FACT

Cool-Hunting Trend Predictions
- Ancient Chinese hairstyle with the upper part of the head shaved and the pony tail in the back like in *The Last Emperor*.
- Wearing underwear outside of the pants so that people know you have clean underwear on.
- Necklaces made from the skulls of captured and executed terrorists.

---

cryptography *(noun)*
The study and practice of hidden and coded language.
How good are you at CRYPTOGRAPHY? Can you make out this code? One of the best cryptographers in the country took less than ten minutes to decipher it. Swedoeigfnedodldsj 111119hjeow 8888eorit.

GEEK FACT

There are many codes that, as of yet, remain undecoded. Examples are Kryptos, a sculpture by Jim Sanborn located at CIA headquarters; some of the letters from the Zodiac killer; and the Beale Papers, nineteenth century coded messages that supposedly lead to a buried treasure worth $40 million.

cryptozoology *(noun)*
The study and pursuit of animals that are considered mythological.
Some mythological animals we have been searching for in CRYPTOZOOLOGY are the dragon, the Loch Ness monster, and a human female who picks up a check.

culture jam *(noun)*
A tactic used in consumer social movements to disrupt mainstream institutions through subvertising or the interruption of broadcast transmissions. Culture jammers believe that images that produce the emotions of shock, shame, fear, and anger will serve as the catalyst for social change.
Yo, we need a CULTURE JAM to stop the war in Afghanistan.

Dark Side of the Rainbow *(proper noun)*
The effect produced when *The Wizard of Oz* is played in sync with Pink Floyd's *Dark Side of the Moon*. The scenes and movements appear to correspond with the sounds of the album.
DARK SIDE OF THE RAINBOW makes the movie fun, but the music is still boring.

decora *(noun)*
Layered clothing, colorful dresses, and over-the-top accessories, including toys, bling, and excessive "flair" à la *Office Space*.
Yo, I gotta get me some DECORA so I can peacock for the ladies tonight, bro.

DEVO *(proper noun)*
The original geek band that scored a huge hit in the eighties with the single "Whip It." Devo's songs often featured science-fiction or surrealist themes tempered by satirical humor. Cofounder Mark Mothersbaugh later went on to compose music for more TV shows than you could crack a whip at.
The name DEVO is a shortened form of "deevolution."

Dunning-Kruger effect *(noun)*
A phenomenon in which people who are unskilled overrate their competence and those who are skilled and capable underrate their competence. This is why stupid people think they are smart.
If it weren't for the DUNNING-KRUGER EFFECT, I'd be out of a job.

dystopia *(noun)*
The opposite of a utopia; a society marked by corruption and poverty and usually under a totalitarian state. Dystopian societies are popular in many science-fiction stories, such as *Akira*, *Blade Runner*, and *1984*.
DYSTOPIAS are popular in Africa. Well, not popular. But numerous.

fanboy or fangirl *(noun)*
A fan whose fanaticism borders on obsession. Usually used in a semiderogatory fashion.
Joss Whedon is not God, FANBOY. Demigod maybe, but not God.

fan fiction *(noun)*
Fiction written by fans rather than by the original creator(s) of a setting or characters. Most fan fiction is "published" on the Internet, since publishers don't like to be sued for copyright infringement.
Most successful authors do not like FAN FICTION because they think it is an infringement upon their work—and it's just plain lazy on the part of would-be writers. Write your own story, fanboy!

fanthropology *(noun)*
The study of fans and what makes them who they are.
Last year a team of FANTHROPOLOGISTS went missing while exploring the deepest parts of the San Diego Comic-Con and were never heard from again.

GEEK QUIZ
What kind of a fan are you?
Have you considered doing any of the following to your favorite star?
❑ Writing
❑ Stalking
❑ Killing . . . Why should he get all the fame? Where's your fifteen minutes, huh?

fanzine *(noun)*

An unofficial small press publication made by fans for a particular interest.

I wonder why my FANZINE based on my love of Arm Fall-Off Boy never gained much interest.

farb *(noun)*

People in historical re-enactments who do not care about being historically accurate or use materials that are too modern.

Lest ye be a FARB, I doth pronounce thus, thou must only speake in ye olde English henceforth.

filk *(noun)*

A type of folk music, first appearing in the 1950s, that has a science-fiction or fantasy theme, created by fans and sung at conventions and filk gatherings.

There is a controversy among fans as to whether 'Weird Al' Yankovic plays FILK music.

flash mob *(noun)*

A crowd gathered in one area at a particular time to perform a pointless act such as pillow fighting or disco dancing without music.

Let's go to the fight. You won't be hurt. It's a FLASH MOB pillow fight!

flesh hunt *(noun)*
A phenomenon that occurs in China. When an anonymous individual posts something on the Internet that incurs the wrath of the people, everyone works to find the person for punishment.
Imagine thousands of people trying to track you down in a FLESH HUNT for uploading a cat-stomping video.

furry *(noun)*
Anthropomorphic animal characters. In furry (or furrydom or furdom), the characters are animals, but they speak, walk on two legs, and are generally human in every way except physical form. An oft-cited example of early furry is Disney's animated *Robin Hood* (the one where Rob is a fox), but most furry aspects have since taken on a decidedly adult tone, creepily so, even by geek standards.
I went to a FURRY convention last year. The nightmares still haven't stopped.

furvert *(noun)*
A furry, or fan of anthropomorphic characters, who is also a pervert.
If your dream girl has fox ears and a tail, then you are a FURVERT.

ganguro *(noun)*
A trend in Japan wherein girls bleach their hair blonde, get orange tans, and wear heavy makeup and bright colors.
Have you seen the show, The Real GANGUROS of Harajuku*?*

geek chic *(noun)*
To purposely embrace geeky fashion and interests, such as wearing black-framed glasses with tape in the middle.
Some NBA athletes in 2010 wore geeky glasses to be GEEK CHIC.

GEEK FACT

Hip to Be Square
It is now hip to be a geek. For years, being an underconfident, socially awkward and introverted intellectual was considered a bad thing. Can you imagine? But now everyone wants to be a geek. Girls with blonde roots, fake tans, breast implants, and a third-grade education can be heard giggling and saying, "I like to read. I am such a geek."

No, you are *not* a geek. Once geeks are trendy, they are not geeks anymore. The new geeks of today are the star quarterbacks of yesteryear.

gothloli *(noun)*
Gothic Lolita. Fashion combining gothic imagery such as crosses, black clothing, and dark makeup with Lolita fashion.
GOTHLOLI is for the more sensitive and brooding perverts.

Hagakure *(proper noun)*
The Book of the Samurai, written by Yamamoto Tsunetomo in the early eighteenth century, gives views on bushido and the code of the samurai. In Jim Jarmusch's film *Ghost Dog*, Forest Whitaker's hit man character obeys the Hagakure very strictly.
The HAGAKURE contains vast amounts of important facts, such as: Did you know that the Last Samurai was Tom Cruise?

Harajuku *(proper noun)*
Distinctive clothing styles such as cosplay or goth Lolita (gothloli) popularized by teenage girls in the Harajuku district of Tokyo.
If you go to HARAJUKU and wear just a tee shirt and jeans you will feel like a loser.

hikikomori *(noun)*
A class of people who are reclusive and uncomfortable with social interactions and choose to lock themselves away. Currently a huge phenomenon in Japan.
Come out of your room, John. It's been two days, you are starting to act like a HIKIKOMORI!

infinite monkey theorem *(noun)*
A theory that if a monkey typed random words for an infinite amount of time it would eventually produce a play by Shakespeare. Featured in *The Simpsons*.
A real study was conducted based on the INFINITE MONKEY THE-OREM by the University of Plymouth in 2003, but the monkey only bashed the typewriter and urinated on it. To pee on a typewriter or not to pee on the typewriter. That is the question.

jeet kune do *(proper noun)*
A martial arts system developed by Bruce Lee that combined many martial arts. The primary principle was "be like water."
JEET KUNE DO is a precursor to MMA because of its integration of many styles according to what is necessary in the situation.

kogal *(noun)*
Fashion involving wearing a Japanese school uniform.
I had my girlfriend dress KOGAL, and it was yummy.

life hack *(verb)*
To use tricks or shortcuts used to make a process easier to understand or complete. Originally coined by computer programmers.
Trying to LIFE HACK a book called Geektionary *would be counterproductive.*

mashup *(noun)*
A combination of different media, such as mixing scenes from a movie with different music or sound.
The Internet has many fake trailers where a movie can be made to resemble Brokeback Mountain *by MASHING the scenes together in a certain way.*

MC Frontalot *(proper noun)*
A hip-hop musician in San Francisco who named the genre known as "nerdcore hip-hop."
My name is MC FRONTALOT. I'm from the streets. I like D&D and chillin' with my fellow geeks. Love the Mac, but prefer the PC, 'cause I can create mad viruses and destroy the infrastructure of the city. Yea, boy!

model robots *(noun)*
Construction kits that allow a person to snap together pieces to create a model mecha, such as Gundam, a popular model robot set. The hobby of collecting model robots is sometimes called *gunpla* in Japan, combining the words "Gundam" and "plastic."
I will conquer the world with my army of MODEL ROBOTS!

netizen *(noun)*
A person who is hooked into the cyberspace community.
Facebook and Myspace are great, but back in the days of AOL chatrooms, every NETIZEN was hooking up.

orkdork *(noun)*
Also known as orchdork, a derogatory term for someone who plays in the school orchestra or band.
In American Pie, *everyone thought that the redhead flute player was an ORKDORK. That is, until she said, "One time, at band camp . . ."* And you know the rest.

pez *(verb)*
To raise one's head very quickly, mimicking the Pez candy dispensers.
I saw this Olivia Munn lookalike and my head was totally like a PEZ, bro.

phantasmagoria *(noun)*
A horror show popular in Europe in the nineteenth century that used projections of ghosts and demons using a magic lantern.
Finish this famous Victorian joke: A priest, a rabbi, and a guy selling a PHANTASMAGORIA show walk into a bar . . .

photobomb *(verb)*
Deliberately appearing in the background of someone else's photo, especially making a funny face, or having someone do the same to yours.
I have mastered the art of PHOTOBOMBING my friends' pictures.

phreak *(noun)*
The subculture of people who are interesting in experimenting, learning about, and taking advantage of telecommunications systems.
You might be a PHREAK if, when you see someone with a better phone, you feel like killing them.
Or if you just looked down from this book to check your BlackBerry.

points of articulation *(noun)*
The rotating joints on an action figure.
Ever since Jimmy collided with another player in a football game, his POINTS OF ARTICULATION haven't been working right.

polyester soldiers *(noun)*
People in historical re-enactments who do not take the time to make their outfits or behavior historically accurate.
I knew he was a POLYESTER SOLDIER when he started talking on his iPhone during the Civil War reenactment.

The Puzzle Palace *(proper noun)*
National Security Agency headquarters.
I work at the PUZZLE PALACE. I'd tell you what I do there, but then I would have to kill you.

retcon *(noun)*
When the history of a fictional universe is changed by its creator(s). A famous retcon is when Arthur Conan Doyle killed off his character Sherlock Holmes and then, responding to popular demand, brought him back to life.
Wanting to milk the franchise for more cash, the writer called in a RETCON.

SCA *(noun)*
Short for Society for Creative Anachronism. A group of people interested in recreating and learning the culture of pre–seventeenth-century Europe.
Methinks that once thou drinketh from the goblet of SCA, thou shalt return from whence ye came.

schwag *(noun)*
Free promotional items and gifts given out at special events such as comic conventions or awards ceremonies. Schwag at the Academy Awards can be worth thousands of dollars.
I got some SCHWAG this weekend—some sample comics and posters from the Comic-Con.

smoot *(noun)*
A nonstandard unit of measurement that began as an MIT fraternity prank. A smoot measures 5'7", which was the height of Oliver Smoot, a fraternity pledge to Lambda Chi Alpha, for which the unit is named. As further proof that geeks are indeed conquering the Earth, one can measure any distance on the planet with Google Earth using miles, kilometers, yards, feet, inches, and smoots.
Most hobbits are well over a half-SMOOT in height.

squidzillionaire *(noun)*
A geek who made massive amounts of money through a project, invention, or website.
Famous SQUIDZILLIONAIREs include Bill Gates, Jeff Bezos, and that guy from Facebook. I hate him!

Stargate Project *(noun)*
A CIA project started in the 1970s to test the psychic abilities of individuals, particularly "remote viewing."
I would love to meet you for a drink, but I really have to finish this STARGATE PROJECT.

GEEK FACT

Confessions of a Geek
According to my father, he is developing a mind-control system based on remote-viewing technology for the STARGATE PROJECT. The system will be able to control the thoughts of all mankind, including world leaders, in order to ensure peace and security throughout the world. Way to go, Pop!

technofreak *(noun)*
A person who is obsessed with technology and must always know everything about and have the latest gadget.
My mother is not a TECHNOFREAK. I gave her an iPhone for Christmas. She asked me what it was.

Thomas Dolby *(proper noun)*
Pop star of the 1980s who had a huge hit with the ultrageeky "She Blinded Me with Science." He later founded a company that makes software synthesizers widely used in mobile phones, and he is also a member of the UK Flat Earth Society.
THOMAS DOLBY, if you really believe the Earth is flat, you may have been blinded, but not by science.

Tsunami *(proper noun)*
Nickname of Takeru Kobayashi, record-setting food-eating champ who can eat more than fifty hot dogs in one sitting.
TSUNAMI is also a member of the International Federation of Competitive Eating (IFOCE).

watermarking *(noun)*
The process of hiding information in a product, usually used to identify the owner of the product.
Digital WATERMARKING was used in detecting the person who leaked the movie Wolverine: Origins *onto the Internet.*

Weezer *(proper noun)*
A popular rock band that is proof positive that geek is the new chic. Frontman Rivers Cuomo is a Harvard graduate who maintains contact with his fans online and likes to play elven or half-elven fighter/thieves in D&D.
Playing D&D while listening to WEEZER . . . is that geek or cool?

World Superhero Registry *(proper noun)*
A community of real-life superheroes with costumes and call signs who engage in vigilantism.
Quick, somebody call the WORLD SUPERHERO REGISTRY!

GEEK FACT

Geekin' Out

If you could be a superhero, who would you be?

Spider-Man
Pro: Get to stick to walls
Con: Have to be played by Tobey Maguire

Batman
Pro: Get to have a kick-ass ride
Con: Bruce Wayne already has a kick-ass ride

Chapter 2

GEEKS IN SPACE: SCIENCE FICTION AND FANTASY

All geeks are intimately familiar with many of these terms—or better be. Geeks have been looking to the heavens for a long time, dreaming of creating new worlds for humankind to explore. Science fiction and fantasy are the perfect expressions of the geek's exploratory mind. If Christopher Columbus were a geek, he would only have written about another world populated with "Indians," not sailed in the wrong direction to kill them. Thus the geek is humankind's most mild-mannered, yet most adventurous explorer. The following terms are taken from geek contributions to sci-fi and fanstasy across a variety of media.

42 *(noun)*
The answer to the ultimate question of life, the universe, and everything, as given by the supercomputer Deep Thought in the *Hitchhiker's Guide to the Galaxy* by Douglas Adams. Deep Thought took 7 million years to come up with that answer.
42 is the Ultimate Answer, but the Ultimate Question is unknown.

GEEK FACT

Possible Ultimate Questions
43-1= ?
What do you get when you reverse the digits of the number 24?
What number do you get when you take the oldest age a woman can still be physically attractive and multiply it by 2?

Alderson Disk *(proper noun)*
A fictional artificial space ring, several thousand miles thick, that has a hole at the center where the sun will be located.
This frosted donut causes my mind to contemplate the vastness and structural beauty of the ALDERSON DISK.

alien space bats *(noun)*
A term used to make fun of plot devices in alternate history stories that create implausible scenarios to make their universe unique.
In Harry Turtledove's World War novels, aliens invade Earth in the middle of World War II. That's so ALIEN SPACE BATS.

alternate history *(noun)*
A genre of science fiction premised upon the concept that historical events might have turned out differently, such as the South winning the Civil War or the Axis Powers winning Word War II. Harry Turtledove is a very popular author of alternate history fiction.
Great ALTERNATIVE HISTORY books: How the West (of Europe) was Won *by Adolf Hitler, bestselling author of* Mein Kampf; The Rise and Fall of Capitalism *by Karl Marx Jr.;* How Rome Never Fell *by current Roman Emperor, Guido Caesar.*

amontillado *(noun)*
A rare and valuable Italian wine used by Edgar Allan Poe in his short story, *The Cask of Amontillado.*
In The Cask of AMONTILLADO, *another light-hearted, hysterical tale of whimsy by Poe, an aggrieved nobleman avenges himself against an enemy by sealing him up brick by brick in the catacombs.*

atompunk *(noun)*
Derivative of cyberpunk, this term deals with the period after World War II concerning the space and arms races and communist paranoia.
The top three consequences of ATOMPUNK are bomb shelters, McCarthyism, and nuclear weapons that kick ass!

Avalon *(proper noun)*
A mythical island in Arthurian legend where Excalibur was created and where King Arthur goes to heal after the Battle of Camlann, and from which he will supposedly return.
AVALON is beautiful this time of year. But housing prices are still through the roof . . .

Azathoth *(proper noun)*
A fictional god in H. P. Lovecraft's Cthulhu mythos, also known as the Blind Idiot God.
I do not worship AZATHOTH. He's just a friend.

balrog *(noun)*
Large monstrous creatures who were servants of Morgoth. One appears in the movie *The Fellowship of the Ring* as a horned beast on fire with a whip that pulls Gandalf down into the chasm.
We have to be quiet when we sneak back into the house or else the BALROG may awaken and try to ground us.

Battle School *(proper noun)*
A military school in *Ender's Game,* a classic science-fiction novel by Orson Scott Card, at which children are taught military strategies and tactics in simulated battles.
My high school is so rough I feel like I'm in BATTLE SCHOOL.

Battletech *(proper noun)*
A science-fiction franchise based on large fighting robots piloted by Mechwarriors. Battletech includes RPGs, video games, and gaming centers where players enter cockpits and pilot robots in multiplayer battles.
I often went to BATTLETECH centers as a kid and became a jaded veteran of the mech wars.

BDO *(noun)*
A big dumb object, as coined by science-fiction writer Larry Niven. It is a giant construction such as Ringworld or the Halo structure in the game *Halo*.
My stepfather was a BDO. Now, he's a BDOF—big dumb object with a felony.

beta reader *(noun)*
A person who reads fan fiction before it is released to gauge its quality and provide feedback.
My story of Batman as a crime-fighting tax accountant did not go over well with my BETA READER.

biopunk *(noun)*
Derivative of cyberpunk but focusing on biotechnology. Also used to describe a biohacker who experiments with DNA.
I could never be a BIOPUNK because I wasn't the biggest fan of biology. What the heck is a mitochondria again?

C. Auguste Dupin *(proper noun)*
Fiction's first detective, who solves the murders of two women by an orangutan in Paris in Edgar Allan Poe's *The Murders in the Rue Morgue*.
C. AUGUSTE DUPIN established the typical detective trope of the eccentric and brilliant detective surrounded by fools.

Clarke's Three Laws *(proper noun)*
Arthur C. Clarke developed three laws of prediction:
1. If an older scientist says that something is possible, he is right; when he says it is impossible, he is probably wrong.
2. The only way to discover the limits of the possible is to venture farther into the impossible.
3. Any "sufficiently advanced technology" cannot be distinguished from magic.
After CLARKE'S THREE LAWS, I realized that an iPhone was pagan magic.

cloaking *(noun)*
Technology-based invisibility. Used in fiction, such as Harry Potter, *Star Trek*, and the movie *Predator*, but has a basis in reality called metamaterial cloaking, which uses metal to bend light around an object.
For Halloween I am CLOAKING just my body so that I'll look like a floating head.

clockpunk *(noun)*
Derivative of cyberpunk but focusing on the technology of clocks.
Riveting. After CLOCKPUNK, what's next, cardboardpunk?

codex *(noun)*
The modern stitched format of books, a replacement of scrolls, developed by the Romans; also the name given to manuscripts from antiquity through the Middle Ages.
The CODEX Gigas *was created in the thirteenth century by a monk who was said to have sold his soul to the devil so that the devil could finish the manuscript. It is also referred to as the* Devil's Bible *because it contains a version of the Bible and has a picture of the devil on one of the pages.*

Conan *(proper noun)*
There are two great Conans in geekdom:
1. A fictional character created by Texan Robert E. Howard. Conan the Barbarian is the primary hero of the sword and sorcery genre and star of many short stories, novels, comic books, movies, and video games.
2. Conan O'Brien, one of the most successful geeks in the entertainment industry, rose to fame as a writer on *Saturday Night Live* and *The Simpsons*, then went on to host his own late-night TV talk show before being PWNed by Jay Leno.
CONAN, what is best in life?

GEEK FACT

What is best in life? At least according to Ahnuld in the movie *Conan the Barbarian:* "Cwush yoah enemies, see them dwiven befoah you, and to hear the wamentation of their women."

2

conlanger *(noun)*

Someone who creates a new "constructed language" (or "conlang"), usually for use in fantasy or science fiction settings. J. R. R. Tolkien is the patron saint of conlangers for his work in creating many languages in *The Lord of the Rings.* Other famous constructed languages are Klingon, Vulcan, and Na'vi.

Once derided by even science-fiction writers, CONLANGERS are now being hired (and paid!) to construct languages for such movies as Avatar *and Disney's* Atlantis.

cosmic horror *(noun)*

A two-part principle devised by H. P. Lovecraft that states:
1. Humans are incapable of understanding life.
2. The universe is alien.

Oh, Horror of horrors, what is this indescribable COSMIC HORROR creature before me that is driving me insane!

GEEK QUOTE

"Grant me one request. Grant me revenge! And if you do not listen, then to hell with you!"

—CONAN PRAYING TO CROM IN THE JOHN MILIUS FILM *CONAN THE BARBARIAN*

Crom *(proper noun)*

A god worshipped by Conan the Barbarian and his Cimmerian people.
By CROM, the one who stole my pudding shall taste my steel!

GEEK FACT

Conan author Robert E. Howard probably got the name from the ancient Celtic god Crom Cruach.

Cthulhu *(proper noun)*
A cosmic being in the H. P. Lovecraft mythos that is terrifying in nature and appearance and is worshipped by a doomsday cult.
CTHULHU is a creature of cosmic horror that is indescribable in terrifying appearance. Think of the body of Rosie O'Donnell with the head of . . . well, Rosie O'Donnell.

cyberpunk *(noun)*
A genre of science fiction focused on technologies such as artificial intelligence, virtual reality, and hacking, usually taking place in a dystopian society. William Gibson's *Neuromancer* is considered the ultimate work of cyberpunk, but cyberpunk has gained more mainstream awareness through movies such as *Blade Runner* and *Johnny Mnemonic*.
A true CYBERPUNK lover rollerblades and wears neon colors.

dark lord *(noun)*
One of the great tropes of fantasy stories. Very often a sorcerer or some sort of evil creature, dark lords are usually bent on world domination or destruction.
Famous DARK LORDS include Morgoth, Sauron, Darth Vader, Dick Cheney, and Doctor Doom.

Death Dealer *(proper noun)*
A shadowy armored character created by Frank Frazetta in an iconic 1973 painting.
While most of Frazetta's paintings took him only one night to complete, DEATH DEALER took three days.

death ray *(noun)*
A weapon that could cause instantaneous death through a particle beam.
Nikola Tesla stated that he had invented a DEATH RAY, called teleforce, but it turned out to be vaporware.

demons *(noun)*
Supernatural beings who tempt and torment humans. In 1589, Peter Binsfeld classified them according to the Seven Deadly Sins: Lucifer: pride; Mammon: greed; Asmodeus: lust; Leviathan: envy; Beelzebub: gluttony; Satan/Amon: wrath; Belphegor: sloth.
I definitely have the DEMON Belphegore in me.

diesel punk *(noun)*
Derivative of cyberpunk but focusing on the technology of the time period just before and around World War II.
DIESEL PUNK has been made obsolete by "Unleaded with Techron Punk."

Discworld *(proper noun)*
The setting of Terry Pratchett's novels about a flat world that is in fact a parody of fantasy tropes.
Thirty-seven DISCWORLD novels have been published.

djinni *(noun)*
Another word for genie, which is a spirit that possesses magical powers and can be either a good or evil influence on humans.
A dinjiinyeh is a female DJINNI.

Eä *(proper noun)*
In J. R. R. Tolkien's mythologies (especially in *The Silmarillion*), Eä is a Quenya (the "High Tongue" of the elves) word for the universe and everything within the universe.
Arda, or Middle-earth, lies within EÄ.

Elric of Melniboné *(proper noun)*
An albino antihero featured in the novels of Michael Moorcock, who is the emperor of Melniboné and wields the sword, Stormbringer, which gives him unique powers but also curses his soul. Elric first appeared in the 1961 novellette "The Dreaming City" and has since been featured in numerous novels, comics, and role-playing games, including Advanced Dungeons & Dragons.
ELRIC OF MELNIBONÉ has been referenced or has appeared in the Conan the Barbarian *comics,* Fullmetal Alchemist, *and* Babylon 5.

Elvish *(noun)*
J. R. R. Tolkien actually created multiple languages spoken by elves and the other residents of Middle-earth. Elvish was spoken in the movie by Liv Tyler and the guy who played Mr. Anderson in *The Matrix*, Hugo Weaving. If you really want to display your geek knowledge, you should know that the two primary types of Elvish in use in the Third Age of Middle-earth are Quenya (inspired by Finnish) and Sindarin (inspired by Welsh).
With the departure of the last ship from the Grey Havens, ELVISH has left the building.

Exegesis *(proper noun)*
A journal by Phillip K. Dick about his hallucinations and theories that the world is a simulated reality.
Many crazy people keep their own version of the EXEGESIS, but I don't because the men in the black helicopters might try to steal it and read my mind.

fafia *(noun)*
"Forced away from it all." The implication is that one would really rather still be involved in fandom, but circumstances make it impossible.
Being gainfully employed and having an active social life are major producers of FAFIA.

fanspeak *(noun)*
The slang and lingo used by fans of sci-fi and fantasy.
FANSPEAK crosses all geographical and linguistic boundaries. Geeks of the world, unite!

fantasy metal *(noun)*
Heavy metal music with lyrics that reference fantasy elements such as *The Lord of the Rings*. Example: Dragonland.
FANTASY METAL rocks when you are fighting a LARP battle.

Finagle's Law *(proper noun)*
A corollary of Murphy's Law used often in science fiction: "Anything that can go wrong, will—at the worst possible moment."
Captain Kirk once told Spock, "As one of FINAGLE'S LAWS puts it: 'Any home port the ship makes will be somebody else's, not mine.'"

Flatland *(proper noun)*
A romance of many dimensions. An 1884 novel by Edwin Abbott about a two-dimensional world and the shapes that inhabit the world, including squares and polygons.
South Dakota is also FLATLAND.

Foundation *(proper noun)*
In the science-fiction series by Isaac Asimov, it is an organization founded by scientists that hopes to preserve civilization during a predicted period of dystopian barbarity. The group uses the science of psychohistory, which allows scientists to predict and affect the future on a long-term, macro level using statistics, computers, and sociology.
A reimagining of FOUNDATION will surely appear in a 3D movie starring Will Smith and directed by Michael Bay.

Fox-Maiden *(noun)*
In ancient Japan, a supernatural female seductress that can change her shape at will.
Medieval Japanese horror stories were fixated upon female ghosts (or obake), female monsters, and FOX-MAIDENS. Another sign that women were revered and respected throughout the ages.

Frank Frazetta *(proper noun)*
An American fantasy and science-fiction artist famed for his paintings of Conan the Barbarian and Jon Carter of Mars. Considered by many geeks to be the greatest fantasy artist of all time.
FRANK FRAZETTA is to geeks as Monet is to snobs.

Frodo *(proper noun)*
A hobbit and the hero of Tolkien's *The Lord of the Rings.*
FRODO lives. (Reportedly a popular graffiti slogan during the height of the Tolkien craze of the late '60s.)

Futurians *(proper noun)*
A group of science-fiction fans in New York from 1939 to 1945, several of whom became writers, including Issac Asimov and Fredrik Pohl.
The FUTURIANS were formed with political intentions and some of the members supported communism.

gafia *(noun)*
"To get away from it all." A term for when a fan leaves fandom intentionally for personal reasons.
GAFIA was first used by Futurian Dick Wilson in the forties.

Gandalf *(proper noun)*
A wizard in Tolkien's *The Hobbit* and *The Lord of the Rings*. The Five
Wizards were each known by a color, and through most of the books, he
is Gandalf the Grey, a wandering meddler with a fondness for the hobbits' pipeweed.

> *"GANDALF? Yes, that's what they used to call me. GANDALF the
> Grey. That was my name."*

GEEK FACT

All true Tolkien geeks should be able to tell you that the wizards
were not magicians or conjurers but were in fact Maiar, sent to
Middle-earth by the Valar to aid in the fight against Sauron. To
nongeeks: Valar = the archangels; Maiar = lesser angels.
  Although only three wizards appear in *The Lord of the Rings*,
there were actually five. The three who appear in the novel are
Gandalf the Grey, Saruman the White, and Radagast the Brown.
There were also the two Blue Wizards, Alatar and Pallando.

garn! *(phrase)*
Cockney term used by less-educated characters including the orc Shagrat
and Ted Sandyman from the scouring of the Shire in *Lord of the Rings*.
Anyone who doesn't know about the scouring of the Shire has not read
the book, only seen the movie.

> *GARN! You maggot! It is obvious from Tolkien's writings that he
> meant for the Balrog to have wings!*

glossopoeia *(noun)*
A word made up by J. R. R. Tolkien that means the construction of languages for artistic purposes. See also *conlanger*.

> *A Princess of Mars is the first fiction in the twentieth century that
> used GLOSSOPOEIA.*

2

The Golden Bough *(proper noun)*

Anthropological study of ancient European religions written in the nineteenth century. Its primary argument was that pre-Christian religions revolved around the worship and sacrifice of a sacred king who dies at harvest and is reincarnated in spring. Supposedly this explains why ancient Europeans were receptive to Christian gospel.

THE GOLDEN BOUGH was a major influence on literature, including fantasy literature, and inspired the Led Zeppelin classic "Stairway to Heaven."

Gondor *(proper noun)*

In the world of J. R. R. Tolkien, a kingdom ruled by men and founded by Isildur and Anarion. In the Third Age, Sauron weakened Gondor, but he was defeated and Aragorn took his rightful place as king.

"If the beacons of GONDOR are lit, Rohan must be ready for war."
—The Lord of the Rings

GEEK QUOTE

"I am Aragorn, son of Arathorn; and if by life or death I can save you, I will." (Best said while holding your sword aloft.)

—ARAGORN, LATER KING ELESSAR THE ELFSTONE

Grand Grimoire *(proper noun)*

A mystical book, also know as *Le Dragon Rouge*, probably published in France in the eighteenth century but variously ascribed to Solomon or a sixteenth-century Egyptian named Alibeck.

GRAND GRIMOIRE details the different hosts of hell and their powers, describing how to enter a pact with them to attain the magician's goals.

griffin *(noun)*

Legendary beast, half lion and half eagle. Taken originally from Greek myths, it appears in the Harry Potter series and also shows up among the gargoyles festooned upon medieval European churches. Also spelled *griffon* and *gryphon*.

Academics believe that the GRIFFIN is based upon dinosaur fossils discovered by the ancient Greeks.

Hanlon's razor *(proper noun)*
A maxim popularized by science-fiction writer Robert A. Heinlein that states: "Never attribute to malice that which is adequately explained by stupidity."
Do you hear that, 9/11 conspiracy theorists? The Bush years can be summed up in two words: "HANLON'S RAZOR."

hard sci-fi *(noun)*
A genre of science fiction where the science is superficially realistic or attempts to be as accurate as possible. Examples include works by Greg Egan and Arthur C. Clarke.
HARD SCI-FI is rare these days as fantasy and soft science fiction are becoming more popular.

hobbit *(noun)*
The "little people" of J. R. R. Tolkien's *The Hobbit* and *The Lord of the Rings*. Hobbits are typified by their small stature, thick-soled and hairy feet, fondness for meals, and shunning of adventures.
"For a guy who's read THE HOBBIT *fourteen times, you're not so dumb." —Dana Whitaker [to Jeremy] on the TV show* Sports Night

holistic detection *(noun)*
A type of detection used by Dirk Gently in *Dirk Gently's Holistic Detective Agency* by Douglas Adams, where to solve the case one must understand the society, as everything is connected.
If real police officers had to use HOLISTIC DETECTION, nothing would ever be solved.

hyperdrive *(noun)*
In Larry Niven's science-fiction world, a faster-than-light drive that allows humans to travel around the galaxy at approximately one light year every three days. As a hard science fiction writer, Niven provided all of his premises, such as a faster-than-light-drive, with a plausible though unrealistic scientific basis. Parodied as ludicrous speed (see Chapter 8: Geekout at the Silver Screen: Television and the Movies) in the movie *Spaceballs*.
Toyota recently discovered HYPERDRIVE technology. Unfortunately, it kicks in unexpectedly, causing many drivers to crash.

Hypnerotomachia Poliphili *(proper noun)*
Published in 1499, supposedly by Francesco Colonna, this book details a dream of the main character, Poliphilo, who wanders through a surreal landscape. It contains seemingly unending descriptions without story, and the character seems to have almost a sexual attraction to architecture. It has some early examples of sequential art, which is used in comic books.

> *After reading the* HYPNEROTOMACHIA POLIPHILI, *I fell asleep on my sofa. That night, I had an erotic dream about my sofa.*

hysterical realism *(noun)*
A literary genre known for being incredibly detailed and absurd.

> *Examples of* HYSTERICAL REALISM *are the works of Thomas Pynchon, Don DeLillo, and David Foster Wallace.*

incubus *(noun)*
A supernatural male being that sneaks into the rooms of sleeping women to have sex with them. In *The City of God*, St. Augustine acknowledges their existence, calling them sylvans and fauns.

> *In ancient times, it might have been useful for an unmarried woman to explain a pregnancy by blaming it upon an* INCUBUS.

jet pack *(noun)*
A device strapped to one's back that allows one to fly, as seen in fiction such as *The Rocketeer* and used in real life by astronauts.

> *Yves Rossy flew his own* JET PACK *across the English Channel.*

The King in Yellow *(proper noun)*
A gothic horror book by Robert W. Chambers that describes a play called *The King in Yellow* where any viewer or reader will be tragically affected. Also in the Cthulu mythology.

> THE KING IN YELLOW *is a nineteenth-century version of* The Ring.

GEEK FACT

"Arda" is the Quenya word for Middle-earth.

Languages of Arda *(proper noun)*
Languages created by J. R. R. Tolkien for use in Middle-earth, derived from many real languages. As a professional philologist (one who studies language), Tolkien had a passion for language, and even invented his first language at age thirteen. See also *Elvish*.
I am fluent in all the LANGUAGES OF ARDA, which is cool but even less useful than speaking French.

The Last Unicorn *(proper noun)*
A novel by Peter S. Beagle and an animated film by Rankin/Bass about a unicorn that thinks she is the last of her kind and her quest to find the rest.
The music for the animated version of THE LAST UNICORN was done by America, the band behind "A Horse with No Name."

locked-room mystery *(noun)*
A mystery story involving a murder that occurs inside a locked room and therefore limits the suspects.
The Swedish novel The Girl with the Dragon Tattoo *is an example of a LOCKED-ROOM MYSTERY because the murderer must have been on an island that had no exit.*

Lord Dunsany *(proper noun)*
An author who was popular in the early twentieth century who established the popularity of the fantasy novel and short story.
LORD DUNSANY influenced Robert E. Howard, H. P. Lovecraft, Jorge Luis Borges, David Eddings, Neil Gaiman, and many others.

metaverse *(noun)*
A term for a virtual reality Internet interface in the book *Snow Crash* by Neal Stephenson.
Welcome to the METAVERSE, my friends. Here you can look however you want. Your avatar can eliminate those unsightly love handles.

Middle-earth *(proper noun)*
"The world" in Tolkien's books, especially *The Hobbit* and *The Lord of the Rings*.
"The battle for MIDDLE-EARTH is about to begin."

Mordred *(proper noun)*
The illegitimate child of King Arthur who betrayed his father and fought him in the Battle of Camlann, leading to Mordred's death and a fatal wound for Arthur.
Never trust a dude named MORDRED. Every Mordred I have ever met was a total tool.

Morgoth *(proper noun)*
The primary dark lord in the world of J. R. R. Tolkien. Comparable to Satan. Sauron (from *The Lord of the Rings*) was Morgoth's lieutenant. Morgoth terrorized the world before being thrown into the Void, as detailed in *The Silmarillion*.
My ex-girlfriend was half Swiss-German and half-MORGOTH.

muggle *(noun)*
A person in the Harry Potter universe who does not possess magical powers.
There is nothing worse than being a MUGGLE like me. My only special power is the ability to touch the tip of my tongue to the tip of my nose.

The Mule *(proper noun)*
From Isaac Asimov's Foundation series, a crossbreed who couldn't have children. As an anomaly, The Mule's actions couldn't be predicted by the First Foundation's calculations.
The MULE is finally defeated by the Second Foundation, who use psychic powers to alter his ambitions.

multiverse *(noun)*
Used heavily in fiction, it is where many different dimensions exist at once, with travel between the worlds. As seen in DC Comics' *Crisis on Infinite Earths*, *The Adventures of Luther Arkwright*, the Elric series by Michael Moorcock, and many other places.
When I get the munchies, I go to the store and travel through the candy MULTIVERSE.

mûmakil *(noun)*
Enormous elephants in Tolkien's *The Lord of the Rings*. Also called oliphaunts and used in Battle of the Pelennor Fields.
We went to see the MÛMAKIL at the Bronx Zoo.

GEEK FACT

"Mûmakil" is the plural usage. Singular is "mûmak."

My Precious *(proper noun)*
In Tolkien's *The Lord of the Rings*, the tormented character Gollum refers to the One Ring as "My Precious." In geekdom, the term refers to anything over which the geek has an unhealthy (perhaps even self-destructive) obsession.
  Ultimate Spider-Man #1 *signed by both Bendis and Bagley! Ohhhhh, MY PRECIOUS.*

mythopoeia *(noun)*
The creation of myth in literature, as seen by J. R. R. Tolkien, who invented his own world and mythology, much of which was never published until years after his death.
  MYTHOPOEIA can be seen as either good preparation or a type of writer's block.

nadsat *(noun)*
The slang used by teenagers in *A Clockwork Orange* by Anthony Burgess. It is a combination of English, Russian, Cockney expressions, Biblical references, a bit of German, and Burgess's imagination. The term "nadsat" itself is taken from the Russian suffix used in the numbers 11 through 19—the English equivalent of which would be "teen." So nadsat is basically "teen speak" for the psychopathic teens of Britain's near future. Sort of like if Johnny Rotten were even more unintelligible.
  Viddy well, little brother, appy polly loggy for taking your eggiweg. Blame my sinnys on the NADSAT.

Nazgûl *(proper noun)*
The Ringwraiths in *The Lord of the Rings*. They were powerful men who were given nine Rings of Power, which took away their humanity and led them to be controlled by Sauron.
  The lord of the NAZGÛL is the Witch-King of Angmar, who can't be killed by a man. Eventually he was killed by a woman. And the death was slow—he got married.

GEEK FACT

The true geek will not only know that the term nazgul is derived from the Black Speech, meaning "ring wraith," but that the proper pronunciation is not NAZ-gull, but NAZG-ool. If you're gonna speak the Black Speech, speak it right!

Necronomicon *(proper noun)*
An ancient book of magic in H. P. Lovecraft's universe. The *Necronomicon* was supposedly written by the Mad Arab Abdul Alhazred and exists in several copies, one of which—the Latin translation by Olaus Wormius—is held in the restricted section of the library of Miskatonic University in Arkham, Massachusetts. References to the book also appear in the movie *Army of Darkness.*
　　I'm going to get a copy of the NECRONOMICON *and conjure up a demon to eat your brain!*

Neuromancer *(proper noun)*
A 1984 novel by William Gibson that started the genre of cyberpunk, about a drug-addicted hacker hired for a job in cyberspace.
　　Over twenty years after NEUROMANCER *and still no immersive virtual reality?*

newspeak *(proper noun)*
From George Orwell's novel *1984*, the artificial reduction of language by the government to remove meaning and turn every concept into a dichotomy, such as good and ungood. The lexicon became diminished as "bad" became "ungood" and "wonderful" became "doubleplusgood."
　　If NEWSPEAK-type changes in language equal changes in the way we think, what will be the long-term impact of texting?

ninjapocalypse *(noun)*
The end of the world, caused by an enormous battle with hundreds of thousands of ninja.
　　The NINJAPOCALYPSE is unlikely perhaps. But it's more likely than the Rapture—and way cooler.

GEEK FACT

Imaginary drugs are common in sci fi. In Frank Herbert's *Dune*, Melange was a drug also known as the "Spice" that could give someone psychic powers as well as prolong one's life. Moloko Plus, from *A Clockwork Orange*, was milk that included hallucinogens and other stimulating ingredients. Substance D, from *A Scanner Darkly*, was called Death, and it induced hallucinations and could split someone's consciousness into two separate parts.

Niven's Laws *(proper noun)*
Coined by science-fiction writer Larry Niven, they are:
1. Never fire a laser at a mirror.
2. Ethics change with technology.
3. The only message in science fiction is that there are other minds that think as well as you do, but differently.
NIVEN'S LAWS also state that Larry Niven will write sci-fi novels until he is 110 years old.

The One Ring, or simply The Ring *(proper noun)*
In Tolkien's *The Lord of the Rings*, a magical ring crafted by the Dark Lord Sauron. It granted its wearer invisibility and the power to dominate the will of others, so much so that it had the potential to allow one to conquer the world. But it also slowly ate away at the wearer's soul.
Frodo failed. Bush has THE RING. (A popular bumper sticker favored by geeks in the early years of the twenty-first century.)

orc *(noun)*
A monstrous creature seen in fantasy and in the world of Tolkien. The source of the word is probably from *Beowulf, orc-nass*, which means "death corpses." There is little difference between orcs and goblins, but they are differentiated early in Tolkien's works, being referred to as "goblins" in *The Hobbit* and "orcs" in *The Lord of the Rings*.
The Uruk-hai are an advanced version of ORCS, created by Saruman by breeding orcs with humans.

O'Toole's corollary of Finagle's Law *(proper noun)*

A maxim, loosely based upon the second law of thermodynamics, and used often by hackers, which states: *"The perversity of the universe tends toward a maximum."*

> *The perversity of O'TOOLE'S COROLLARY OF FINAGLE'S LAW is how long the name of the law is.*

panopticon *(noun)*

A type of theoretical prison popular in science fiction where observed prisoners do not see their captors and therefore feel an invisible omnipresence, affecting them psychologically.

> *There are many PANOPTICON-inspired prisons throughout the world, like the modern office cubicle.*

parallel universe *(noun)*

An alternate universe that exists side by side with our universe, only with certain changes that make for an interesting story.

> *PARALLEL UNIVERSES include Narnia, Wonderland, and the Jersey Shore.*

Picts *(proper noun)*

A tribal race of people that were often included in tales from Robert E. Howard. Their king is Bran Mak Morn, a recurring hero in Howard's stories.

> *PICTS were a real people who are famous for painting themselves blue before they fought. They so terrified the Romans that the Emperor Hadrian built a wall across Britain to try to keep the Picts in Scotland.*

Poe Toaster *(proper noun)*

An annual visitor to Edgar Allan Poe's grave, who made the pilgrimage to the writer's last resting place from 1949 to 2009.

> *The POE TOASTER may have actually been several individuals or even a hoax to raise money where the graveyard was located.*

positronic *(adjective)*

Inspired by the then newly discovered positron particle, science-fiction genius Isaac Asimov wrote about a positronic brain that provided consciousness and sometimes telepathic abilities to advanced robots.

> *Commander Data on* Star Trek: The Next Generation *has a POSITRONIC brain.*

post-Potter depression *(noun)*
The depression that comes after finishing the last book in the Harry Potter series.

After being diagnosed with POST-POTTER DEPRESSION, the doctor prescribed some Percy Jackson & The Olympians.

quidditch *(noun)*
A fictional sport in the Harry Potter universe where wizards and witches fly on broomsticks and hit balls into ring-shaped goals.

QUIDDITCH is like polo for geeks. All those witches and wizards zipping around the sky. What could be better than that? Besides shuffleboard, of course.

ray gun *(noun)*
An energy weapon that appears in various guises throughout science fiction. In *Star Wars*, it is a blaster, in *Star* Trek it is a phaser, and in *The War of the Worlds* it is a heat ray.

Artists work to make metal sculptures of RAY GUNS that are incredibly detailed and available for purchase.

Ringworld *(proper noun)*
In Larry Niven's universe, Ringworld is an artificial ring in outer space that spins around, creating gravity, with people living within the inner area of the ring. Ringworld is the model of the big dumb object (BDO) of science-fiction novels and was the inspiration for Halo's smaller rings.

RINGWORLD is like a big space donut. Mmmm...donuts...

Sauron *(proper noun)*
The main antagonist in *The Lord of the Rings*, the dark lord who sets out to rule Middle-earth. His name means "abhorred."

The principal rules over the school just like SAURON.

scrith *(noun)*
The artificial material of which Ringworld is built. It provides protection equivalent to nearly a light year's width of lead and strength comparable to the strong nuclear force.

Target offers the best prices on SCRITH. About $1 a square foot.

The Seven Commandments of Animalism *(proper noun)*
From George Orwell's *Animal Farm*. The revolutionary maxims include:
1. "Whatever goes upon two legs is an enemy."
2. "Whatever goes upon four legs, or has wings, is a friend."
3. "No animal shall wear clothes."
4. "No animal shall sleep in a bed."
5. "No animal shall drink alcohol."
6. "No animal shall kill any other animal."
7. And most famously, the seventh commandment: "All animals are equal."
Once the pigs took over the farm, they changed the last of the SEVEN COMMANDMENTS OF ANIMALISM to: "All animals are equal, but some are more equal than others."

Smaug *(proper noun)*
The dragon in J. R. R. Tolkien's *The Hobbit* that has taken over the Lonely Mountain near the lake city of Dale and lives in the mountain with his treasure. Bilbo, the dwarves, and Gandalf set out on a quest to kill the dragon and reclaim the mountain.
SMAUG's eyes are hypnotic in nature and would have hypnotized Bilbo if he hadn't been invisible using the ring.

GEEK FACT

A true geek will know that the name is *not* pronounced "SMOG" (like the general atmosphere of Los Angeles) but "SMAWG" (rhymes with "loud").

space elevator *(noun)*
A concept devised by Arthur C. Clarke that consists of an extremely long cable extending from Earth to an object in geosynchronous orbit. It cannot be built today, but it is theoretically possible.
Going up on the SPACE ELEVATOR, huh? Another Monday morning. Another day, another dollar.

space-time continuum *(noun)*
The timeline of the universe, starting with the Big Bang. The continuum cannot be disturbed, or it may result in an alternate continuum or destroy the universe by paradox.

Doc Brown and Marty made a couple of adjustments to the SPACE-TIME CONTINUUM.

speculative fiction *(noun)*
A broad genre including science fiction, fantasy, horror, and supernatural fiction. Robert A. Heinlein is believed to have invented the term as an alternative to "science fiction." It is most often used today by geek snobs who wish to distance themselves from the term "science fiction."

I wonder how many SPECULATIVE FICTION books made the New York Times *bestseller list last year? Ah, I could only speculate LOL! LMAO!*

steampunk *(noun)*
A genre of science fiction based on an alternate history where Victorian era steam technology has advanced to a highly developed state. It often includes steam-powered airships, mechanical computers, and robots.

An example of STEAMPUNK is a steam-powered colonist robot. Just add some steam and this European robot will go to any third world country, rape it of its resources, and enslave the population for you. No need to get your hands dirty. Get a steam-powered colonist robot today!

succubus *(noun)*
A very ancient type of supernatural female demon, dating from the ancient Mesopotamians but having popular acceptance in Europe in the Middle Ages. Her calling card is that she sneaks into the rooms of sleeping men and has sex with them. It is believed the succubus was invented to provide an explanation to the occurrence of nocturnal emissions.

Every time I fall asleep at night, I pray for a SUCCUBUS to find my room.

sword and planet *(noun)*

A subgenre of fantasy. Romantic adventures that take place on another planet but with minimal technology. A prime example is *A Princess of Mars* by Edgar Rice Burroughs.

> *SWORD AND PLANET is much more interesting than spoon and planet.*

sword and sorcery *(noun)*

A subgenre of fantasy. Romantic adventures typified by action, suspense, action, magic, and yet even more action. The prime example by which all others are judged are Robert E. Howard's stories, especially those featuring Conan the Barbarian.

> *The novels of Tolkien defined epic fantasy, but it was Howard's Conan who defined SWORD AND SORCERY.*

tanj! *(phrase)*

A swear word used in the science-fiction series Ringworld that is based upon Robert A. Heinlein's complaint, "There ain't no justice!"

> *I make the money and she spends it all. TANJ!*

teleportation *(noun)*

The transfer of matter from one place to the next, usually using some sort of device, like the Stargate or the transporter in *Star Trek*.

> *Make sure you have a bug zapper in your TELEPORTATION DEVICE. Ever seen* The Fly*?*

GEEK FACT

Best Places to Be Teleported
Girls' locker room
Wherever Oliva Munn is
San Diego Comic-Con

Worst Places to Be Teleported
Men's locker room
A Gallagher performance
High school

thoughtcrime *(noun)*
A criminal thought from George Orwell's *1984*, based upon totalitarian practices in the USSR in the 1930s.
"THOUGHTCRIME does not entail death; thoughtcrime is death."

Three Laws of Robotics *(proper noun)*
Used in the fiction of Isaac Asimov, the laws are rules programmed into every robot.
1. A robot may not injure a human being or, through inaction, allow a human being to come to harm.
2. A robot must obey any orders given to it by human beings, except where such orders would conflict with the First Law.
3. A robot must protect its own existence as long as such protection does not conflict with the First or Second Law.
These LAWS OF ROBOTICS make sense. Wish I could get my wife to follow them.

Timeless Halls *(proper noun)*
In the mythology written by Tolkien for Middle-earth, the Timeless Halls are similar to heaven as they are outside the universe and home to God, or Eru.
I will smite thee, and send thee to the TIMELESS HALLS.

trope *(noun)*
A common element within a genre of literature or any other form of entertainment.
TROPES in Fantasy include the hero, the quest, the dark lord, and the special talisman giving the hero special powers.

turtle *(noun)*
In science, Stephen Hawking used the phrase "turtles all the way down" to explain the infinite regression in the universe.
A TURTLE is a cosmic entity in the Stephen King universe, mentioned as an enemy of the villain It. A TURTLE is what Discworld sits upon.

undead *(noun)*
The dead who rise again, usually by supernatural means and with a thirst for blood or hunger for human flesh. (Brains being a particular favorite.)
Popular examples of the UNDEAD are vampires, zombies, and Joan Rivers.

VALIS *(proper noun)*
Short for Vast Active Living Intelligence System. A satellite that sends an information beam into Horselover Fat's brain (a character based on Phillip K. Dick in the novel *VALIS*) telling him god's true nature and that the Roman Empire never ended.
It is rumored that Phillip K. Dick suffered from hallucinations, which often inspired his work. Anyone who doubts it just needs to read VALIS.

The Void *(proper noun)*
In the mythology created by Tolkien for Middle-earth, the Void is the region that is outside of reality and is only encompassed by nothingness. Morgoth was chained and placed in the Void after being defeated by the Valar.
I hear THE VOID is nice this time of year.

warg *(noun)*
A wolf in Norse mythology, also seen in *The Lord of the Rings* as giant wolves ridden by orcs. Wargs are also seen in D&D, *World of Warcraft*, and *Everquest*.
Who's afraid of the big, bad WARG?

wormhole *(noun)*
A path leading through space-time that allows one to travel through universes or through time.
The TV series Star Trek: Deep Space Nine *featured a space station that guarded a stable WORMHOLE.*

zombies *(noun)*
Humans raised from the dead with the desire to feed on brains. Zombies were popularized in the movie *Night of the Living Dead* directed by George Romero. Add zombies to anything and it is cool. Zombie mailman, instant success.

Upcoming ZOMBIE parodies: Desperate House Zombies, The Secret . . . with Zombies!, Everybody Eats Raymond, Debbie Does Zombies, *and* Eat, Drink, Man, Zombie.

GEEK FACT

Zombies originated in voodoo. And if you want to know more than that . . . hey, this is the *Geektionary*, not Wikipedia.

Chapter 3

GEEKS HELP BATMAN FIGHT THE JOKER: COMIC BOOKS

An exhaustive list of comic book terms, characters, creators, artists, and publishers could easily fill several books. But the following terms should provide any nongeek with a working knowledge of the comic book world and keep you from looking like a total noob when your boyfriend drags you to the San Diego Comic-Con.

Some people denigrate comic book heroes, but in Greek and Roman times, people worshipped a large pantheon of gods with super powers. Many comic book heroes, in fact, were based on ancient gods. The Flash was based upon Mercury, Wonder Woman upon Athena and, of course, Thor upon Thor. Taking this concept farther, Superman can be seen as Zeus, but with an Achille's heel—Kryptonite. So, we are not just comic book geeks, we are mythologists!

24-hour comic *(noun)*
A comic book that is written and illustrated within twenty-four hours. Comic artists participate as a group in yearly challenges.

For speed readers who want to move past the 24-HOUR COMIC, they are introducing the 24-second comic.

adamantium *(noun)*
A metal in the Marvel Universe that is unbreakable. It was introduced in 1969 and was discovered in an attempt to recreate the properties of Captain America's shield. The most famous use was the Weapon X Project's success in lacing Wolverine's skeleton with adamantium and giving him adamantium claws.

I have been working out for months, and I still can't seem to bend ADAMANTIUM.

Age of Apocalypse *(proper noun)*
A story in the Marvel Universe that contemplates what would have happened if Professor X had been killed and the supervillain Apocalypse had taken over the world.

In the AGE OF APOCALYPSE, Peter Parker died before becoming Spider-Man.

Alan Moore *(proper noun)*
A legendary British comic book author known for creating *Watchmen, V for Vendetta, The League of Extraordinary Gentlemen, From Hell,* and *The Killing Joke.* He is also known for being a neopagan, an anarchist, and for having an extreme hatred for Hollywood adaptations of his comics.

"I despise the comic industry, but I will always love the comic medium."—ALAN MOORE

Alfred E. Neuman *(proper noun)*
Care-free ginger-headed mascot of *Mad* magazine whose image actually originated in the early 1900s as a commonly used face. His catchphrase is, "What, me worry?"

"It's often been said that I share the politics of Alfred E. Smith and the ears of ALFRED E. NEUMAN." —Barack Obama

animist *(noun)*
One of Scott McCloud's "four tribes" of comics, described in his influential book *Making Comics*. An animist is an instinctual comic creator concerned mainly with the emotion, content, and connection with the reader.
Examples of ANIMISTS include Jack Kirby and Jeff Smith.

Anti-Life Equation *(proper noun)*
The equation that Darkseid (one of the New Gods, a group of cosmic characters created by Jack Kirby) is searching for and is the reason he has come to Earth. If he discovers the equation, he can control all sentient races by proving to them that hope and freedom do not exist.
The ANTI-LIFE EQUATION hopefully doesn't involve calculus or it may be too hard for most people to understand.

Arseface *(proper noun)*
A character in the *Preacher* comic series who was a teenager that used a shotgun on his own face in a failed suicide attempt and came out looking like, well, an arseface.
Hey, ARSEFACE, your face makes the Toxic Avenger look like the dreamy Hal Jordan.

GEEK QUIZ

Every fan dreams of having his or her favorite comic turned into a movie. My dream is for *Preacher* to become a movie. Which of the following comics has *not* been adapted into a live-action movie?

a. *Tintin*

b. *Blondie*

c. *Swamp Thing*

d. *The Tick*

Answer: d (*The Tick* has been adapted both as a Saturday morning cartoon and a live-action TV series.)

Asteroid M *(proper noun)*
The headquarters of the X-Men's foe, Magneto. It was converted to Utopia, an escape for mutants.

ASTEROID M was chosen by Magneto for its excellent school district.

Aunt Petunia *(proper noun)*
The often-mentioned aunt of Ben Grimm (the Thing in the Fantastic Four), who with her husband raised Ben after his parents died.

"That's right. It's the Thing—AUNT PETUNIA'S favorite blue-eyed nephew!"

bamf *(noun)*
The sound that Marvel character and X-Man Nightcrawler makes when he teleports.

If you hear a BAMF, you are already dead.

Batman *(proper noun)*
Batman, also known as "the Caped Crusader" and "the Dark Knight," fights crime wearing a bat-like costume. He possesses no super powers, but uses his high intelligence, powers of detection, martial arts, and gadgets afforded to him by his true identity, billionaire playboy Bruce Wayne, to fight crime in Gotham City against the likes of the Joker, the Penguin, Two-Face, and Catwoman.

The name of Bruce Wayne, BATMAN's secret identity, was originally derived from Robert the Bruce (as seen in Braveheart*) and Anthony Wayne, a hero of the American Revolutionary War.*

Bizarro World *(proper noun)*
A cube-shaped planet where Bizarro Superman lives and where everything is the opposite of that on Earth. To geeks, it is often used as a reference when the world has seemingly gone mad.

> *"Bizarro Superman, Superman's exact opposite, . . .lives in the backwards BIZARRO WORLD. Up is down, down is up, he says hello when he leaves, goodbye when he arrives."*
> *"Shouldn't he say badbye? Isn't that the opposite of goodbye?"*
> *"No, it's still goodbye."*
> *"Does he live underwater?"*
> *"No."*
> *"Is he black?"*
> *"Look, just forget the whole thing."*
> —Elaine and Jerry in *Seinfeld*

Bloodstar *(proper noun)*
The first graphic novel to call itself a "graphic novel," published in 1976, based on a story by Robert E. Howard and illustrated by Richard Corben.

> BLOODSTAR *is the greatest translation of Robert E. Howard ever created.*

Bongo *(proper noun)*
A character in Matt Groening's *Life in Hell* comic that is a white bunny with only one ear. Bongo comics, the company that publishes *The Simpsons* comics, is named after the character."

> *Like BONGO, I believe that school, life, and everything just plain sucks.*

> ## GEEK FACT
> **Bongo's mother:**
> "Cheer up kid. These are the best damn days of your life."
> **Bongo:**
> "You mean it gets worse?"

Bottle City of Kandor *(noun)*
The former capital of Krypton, it was shrunk, and taken by Braniac.
> THE BOTTLE CITY OF KANDOR *was eventually regrown to its normal size and placed on another planet that had a red sun.*

BPRD *(proper noun)*
Bureau for Paranormal Research and Defense in the *Hellboy* comic books. An organization that employs Hellboy and investigates and fights occult and supernatural entities.
> *Hellboy was found by Professor Trevor "Broom" Bruttenholm and raised by the United States Army and the BPRD.*

Bronze Age *(proper noun)*
The period of comics from early 1970s to mid 1980s. Conan the Barbarian and Luke Cage first appeared in comic books in the Bronze Age.
> *The BRONZE AGE is marked by darker stories that dealt with more real world themes such as racism and drug abuse.*

Calvin and Hobbes *(proper noun)*
A syndicated comic strip written and drawn by Bill Watterson that ran in newspapers from 1985 to 1995. It was lauded by critics and became the single-most popular comic strip of the late 1980s and early '90s. The strip followed the exploits of six-year-old Calvin and his stuffed tiger Calvin.
> CALVIN and HOBBES *is the greatest comic strip ever. Ever!*

Calvinball *(noun)*
A game created by Calvin and Hobbes using masks and a croquet set where the rules are made up as the game is played.
> *Let's play CALVINBALL. Okay, whoever types this sentence wins. I win.*

Captain America *(proper noun)*
A Marvel hero created by Joe Simon and Jack Kirby in 1941. He was a soldier named Steve Rogers who, with the aid of a serum giving him special abilities and an indestructible shield, fought for the Allies against the Axis in World War II. After being frozen in ice in suspended animation, he was eventually freed and ended up joining the Avengers.
> *CAPTAIN AMERICA'S shield appears as an "easter egg" in* Iron Man 2.

Cerebro *(proper noun)*
A machine created by Professor Charles Xavier to be able to find mutants around the world. It has actually had its name changed to Cerebra in more recent comic books.
I'm not your CEREBRO, bro.

Cerebus *(proper noun)*
A comic book by Dave Sim about an aardvark that spanned 300 issues and was epic in scale and story.
CEREBUS *is hands-down one of the best tales ever told about a heroic aardvark.*

GEEK FACT

Cerebus the aardvark should not be confused with Cerberus, the three-headed dog who guards the gates of Hades in Greek mythology. Linguists have reconstructed the original meaning of the name Cerebus from its Proto-Indo-European root *ker-beros*, which means "spotted." So Cerberus, the feared three-headed hound who watches over the gates of hell, answers to the name "Spot."

---

classicist *(noun)*
One of Scott McCloud's "four tribes" of comics described in his influential book *Making Comics*. A classicist believes in achieving greatness in comics and desires objective standards of good and evil.
Examples of CLASSICISTS include Neil Gaiman and Frank Cho.

CCA *(proper noun)*
Comics Code Authority. Originated as a response to the gore and violence in 1950s crime and horror comics, the CCA authorized comic books as being "acceptable" under their standards of content. Marvel Comics famously broke the code in 1971 with the publication of *The Amazing Spider-Man* #96–98, their famous "anti-drug" storyline.
Mr. President, the comic books sold today are out of control. We must call in the CCA right away!

Classics Comics *(noun)*

Baby boomers will recall this comic book series that took public domain novels like *Robin Hood* and *Huckleberry Finn* and put them into comic book form for young readers, who then used them as source material for their book reports.

The CLASSIC COMICS version of In Search of Lost Time *by Marcel Proust would be one hundred times longer than* Watchmen.

closure *(noun)*

A Scott McCloud term, defined in *Understanding Comics*, for what the mind does when it fills in the gaps between panels.

CLOSURE is the comic book geek equivalent of yada-yada-yada.

Comic-Con *(noun)*

Short for the San Diego Comic-Con International. A large convention that began as a gathering for comic book fans and creators but has since grown to include movies, television, video games, and anything and everything in popular entertainment. Fans and producers of movies, television, comic books, and other media converge to promote and buy/sell products, meet the stars, and attend discussion panels. Events such as actor appearances, book signings, and upcoming movie sneak peaks are regular Comic-Con occurrences. Other hobbies have their own types of cons.

Catholics go to Rome, Jews to Jerusalem, Muslims to Mecca, capitalists to Wall Street, and geeks go to COMIC-CON.

Comics Guaranty *(proper noun)*

Also known as CGC, it is a third party that gives grades on the quality and value of a comic book, which has an influence in determining the value of a comic book.

I'm afraid of getting my comics graded through the COMICS GUARANTY because they might say they're not worth as much as I would like.

Comiket *(proper noun)*

The largest self-published comic convention in the world. Currently held twice a year in Japan.

I met this catgirl at COMIKET last year. To make a long story short, I now have six kittens to worry about. Kitten support payments are just killing me.

cosmic rays *(noun)*
Interstellar radiation that has transformative powers, including changing Reed Richards, Susan Storm, Johnny Storm, and Ben Grimm into the Fantastic Four.

COSMIC RAYS must be the explanation for that third arm I sprouted.

3

Creator's Bill of Rights *(proper noun)*
Developed by a group of comic creators in the hopes of looking out for their rights and to stop exploitation by corporations in work-for-hire situations.

Jack Kirby had a dispute with Marvel over ownership of original art, one of the issues that led to the CREATOR'S BILL OF RIGHTS.

crossover *(noun)*
When two fictional universes (usually in a comic book) share the same story line.

Famous CROSSOVERS include Archie vs. Punisher, Image vs. Valiant, and Jerry Seinfeld vs. Lady Gaga.

Danger Room *(proper noun)*
A training room for the X-Men that uses holographic projections and energy weapons to train the X-Men in various combat situations. The Danger Room eventually turned sentient. Sadly, the Jungle Room at Graceland has not.

Never stuff yourself on nachos and enter the DANGER ROOM. Bamf or no bamf . . . not a good idea.

The Dark Knight Returns *(proper noun)*
A revolutionary comic book series by Frank Miller, it tells the story of a middle-aged Batman in a dystopian future. Along with *Watchmen*, it is considered the seminal work of Modern Age comics and is credited with popularizing more mature themes in comic books.

THE DARK KNIGHT RETURNS . . . one of the greatest comics ever made. Its sequel, The Dark Knight Strikes Again . . . *epic fail.*

Dark Phoenix *(proper noun)*
A story in the X-Men comic books about Jean Grey (also known as "Marvel Girl") whose attainment of additional powers made her increasingly dangerous. Dark Phoenix, as seen in the third *X-Men* movie, was responsible for the anticlimactic deaths of Cyclops and Professor X.

Don't judge DARK PHOENIX by the X-Men 3 *movie. Trust me. Read the comic.*

DCAU *(proper noun)*
Short for DC Animated Universe. A term used to describe the continuity of the Warner Bros animated series, including *Batman: The Animated Series* and *Superman: The Animated Series*, that were produced by Bruce Timm and Paul Dini.

The DCAU is some people's biggest exposure to the DC Universe.

DC Comics *(proper noun)*
One of the two most prominent comic book publishers (the other being Marvel). DC originally stood for "Detective Comics" (Batman's prime title). DC Comics publishes such classic super heroes as Superman, Batman, and Wonder Woman. DC Comics are also characterized by their iconic heroes and semifictional settings (Metropolis and Gotham rather than New York).

DC COMICS . . . Marvel Comics . . . two great tastes that taste great together.

Deadpool *(proper noun)*
A popular super-powered mercenary character in the Marvel Universe that wears red and black. Created by Rob Liefield, Deadpool has a wisecracking personality and a deformed face.

DEADPOOL is known as "the merc with a mouth."

decompression *(noun)*
A type of storytelling characterized by heavy emphasis on visual emotion in the art over dialogue, character interaction, and more realistic dialogue, which often lead to slower-moving plots. It has sometimes been said that decompression is "writing comics like movies."

Brian Michael Bendis has been both damned and praised for his DECOMPRESSION of Spidey in Ultimate Spider-Man.

Demon in a Bottle *(proper noun)*

A story line from *Iron Man* that focuses on Tony Stark's problems with alcohol. It has become the quintessential Iron Man story.

The DEMON IN A BOTTLE storyline has been alluded to in the Iron Man *movies.*

Dream *(proper noun)*

The main character in DC Comics' *Sandman* series by Neil Gaiman. Dream is the ruler of all dreams.

DREAM is dreaming personified.

EC Comics *(proper noun)*

"Entertaining Comics," which were comics in the 1940s and 1950s that dealt with horror, crime, and science-fiction stories. *Two-Fisted Tales, Tales from the Crypt,* and *Weird Fantasy* were so sexually explicit and gory that the Comics Code Authority was established.

Surprisingly, EC COMICS began as "Educational Comics" and printed Bible stories.

Elfquest *(proper noun)*

A popular comic created by Richard and Wendy Pini in 1978 about a tribe of warrior elves called the Wolfriders and their experiences on a planet with two moons.

ELFQUEST is known for its liberal views, as most tribes are led by women, and generally, the elves are sexually open and unafraid of nudity.

GEEK FACT

Science Fiction and Fantasy worlds often have their own deities. Gan is the God in Stephen King's universe, as mentioned in the Dark Tower series, the One-Above-All is God in the Marvel universe, Arceus is the original Pokemon that created the universe, and Primus is the creator of the Transformers.

---

embellisher *(noun)*

The inker of a comic book that goes to work after the penciler has drawn the comic. During the Golden Age of comics, credits were sparse and important and prolific embellishers often were not credited.

> *My girlfriend calls me a liar. I call myself an EMBELLISHER. Different folks, different strokes.*

Excelsior! *(phrase)*

Even though this term may refer to a poem by Walt Whitman, another poem by Longellow, or a short story by P. G. Wodehouse, the true geek knows that "Excelsior!" is the famous catch phrase of Stan Lee, meaning "ever higher," with which he ended each entry of his column, "Bullpen Bulletins." A secondary geek meaning is the Excelsior class of starship in *Star Trek*.

> *EXCELSIOR!*
> *That's what she said.*

Fallout Boy *(proper noun)*

A.k.a. Rod Runtledge, Radioactive Man's sidekick, as seen in *The Simpsons*, and also the name of a rock band. Fallout Boy gained his powers by being in physical contact with Radioactive Man when he was exposed to his radiation and therefore received a small amount of his powers.

> *The band FALLOUT BOY got its name when they asked an audience for band name suggestions and an audience member shouted, "Fallout Boy."*

GEEK QUIZ

Wolverine's second appearance is in *Giant Size X-Men* #1. (I should know because I own that comic.) In the first appearance of Wolverine, in *The Incredible Hulk* #180 in 1974, what is the result of his first fight with the Incredible Hulk?

a. Wolverine wins

b. The Incredible Hulk wins

c. They knock each other out

d. They decide to settle it over a game of Fizzbin

Answer: c

Famous Funnies *(proper noun)*
Considered to be the first true American comic book, published in 1933.
>   *Did you check out that* FAMOUS FUNNIES *comic book? Boy, that Mutt and Jeff sure are rapscallions!*

The Far Side *(proper noun)*
A popular and hilarious comic by Gary Larson that ran in newspapers from 1980 to 1995. It was only a single-panel and usually involved absurd situations and gags involving dogs, cows, ducks, monsters, aliens, cavemen, and bearded castaways on desert islands.
>   *Best* FAR SIDE *ever? "Cow poetry."*

featureless void *(noun)*
In a comic, this occurs when the characters are floating in a panel with no background, such as in a *Family Circus* comic strip.
>   *If the characters knew they were in a FEATURELESS VOID, would they suffer from an existential crisis?*

flatter *(noun)*
A person who helps to create a comic by using Adobe Photoshop to fill objects with a color so they become "flats" that the colorist can then color.
>   *They may not have as glamorous of a job as a penciler, but a FLATTER is an important role.*

formalist *(noun)*
One of Scott McCloud's "four tribes" of comics, described in his influential book *Making Comics*. A formalist is an experimenter who loves to discuss comics and obsesses in details.
>   *Examples of FORMALISTS include Scott McCloud and Chris Ware.*

fastball special *(noun)*
A signature battle move of Colossus and Wolverine of the X-Men, in which the super-strong Colossus throws the super-mean Wolverine into the midst of their enemies.
>   *The first use of the FASTBALL SPECIAL occurred in* Uncanny X-Men #100.

Fortress of Solitude *(proper noun)*
Superman's headquarters located in the Arctic. It first appeared in 1958 and includes an alien zoo, a chess-playing robot, and central heating.

What is your FORTRESS OF SOLITUDE? Everyone needs a special place to rejuvenate. A place to rest in solace and peace. Is it under your favorite shady tree? A rock by the sea? On top of a giant peach?

gamma rays *(noun)*
Radiation that has transformative powers, including changing Bruce Banner into the Incredible Hulk. It also allows purple pants to have super strength. Unlike many energies and powers in comic books (see also *power cosmic*), gamma rays are real.

The most powerful rays other than GAMMA RAYS are cosmic rays, ultraviolet rays, X-rays, and Ray Romano.

Ghost World *(proper noun)*
A cult classic comic book by David Clowes (also made into a movie), about two alternative teenage girls after they graduate from high school.

The movie version of GHOST WORLD is good because it has Scarlett Johansson.

GEEK QUIZ

Stan Lee has made a cameo in almost every Marvel movie because he is the cocreator of most of the popular characters in the Marvel Universe, such as Spider-Man and the X-Men. What comic character did Stan Lee *not* have a hand in the creation of?

a. Thor

b. Dr. Strange

c. Ego the Living Planet

d. Namor the Sub-Mariner

Answer: d

GhouLunatics *(proper noun)*
The cackling and humorous rotting corpse hosts of the comic books *Tales from the Crypt*, *The Vault of Horror*, and *The Haunt of Fear*. The Ghou-Lunatics included the Cryptkeeper, the Old Witch, and the Vault Keeper.
In a very special issue of the GHOULUNATICS, the Old Witch runs to the airport to embrace the Cryptkeeper only to find he is now in a relationship with the Vault Keeper.

3

Girls of Old Town *(proper noun)*
Prostitutes in the world of *Sin City* that govern and enforce the area themselves without the help of the police.
In the Sin City *movie, the GIRLS OF OLD TOWN fight back against the mob with Clive Owen.*

Golden Age *(proper noun)*
The period of comic books from the late 1930s to the early 1950s. It was during this time that the modern comic book format first appeared, resulting in a rise in popularity, and the superhero genre began to dominate comic books. Popular characters who first appeared in the Golden Age include Superman, Batman, Wonder Woman, and Captain America.
The GOLDEN AGE is also when some famous non-superheroes made their first appearance, such as Archie and his friends.

GEEK FACT

Other Golden Ages in History
Dutch Golden Age 1600–1700
Hollywood Golden Age 1920s–1950s
Spanish Golden Age 1500–1700
English Golden Age 1550–1650
Nazi Golden Age 1933–1945

---

graphic novel *(noun)*
A comic book that is longer in format and covers a larger story. They are also usually more adult and experimental in their themes.
Comic books? Do I look like a peasant to you? Good sir, I only read GRAPHIC NOVELS.

grawlix *(noun)*

The term to describe how swear words are shown in comic strips: with a list of typographical symbols such as @#$%&!!!!. The term was first coined by Mort Walker, creator of *Hi and Lois* and *Beetle Bailey.*

A comic-strip version of the movie Goodfellas *would be half GRAWLIX.*

The Great Cow Race *(proper noun)*

A race in the series *Bone* where many cows race against each other and that Phoney and Smiley Bone try to fix.

Spoiler Alert: The mystery cow in THE GREAT COW RACE is really Smiley Bone in a cow costume.

The Green *(proper noun)*

An elemental community that unites all plants, first seen in Alan Moore's version of *Swamp Thing.*

THE GREEN is that special place we all enter after treating our arthritis with a little doctor-prescribed THC.

Hammerstein *(proper noun)*

Leader of the *ABC Warriors*, a comic by Pat Mills about war robots. He appeared in the Judge Dredd movie.

Thank God for the appearance of the HAMMERSTEIN in Judge Dredd. *Anything to distract the viewer from Sylvester Stallone is a good thing.*

headlights *(noun)*

Large breasts in comic book female characters, as reported in *Seduction of the Innocent*, a 1954 book by Fredric Wertham on the scandalous nature of comic books.

Holy mackerel! Check out the HEADLIGHTS on Wonder Woman!

Hellboy *(proper noun)*

A comic book hero created by Mike Mignola. Hellboy is a demon whose true name is Anung Un Rama. He was summoned by Nazi occultists but rescued by Allied agents in World War II. Raised as a Catholic by Professor Trevor Bruttenholm (pronounced "Broom"), Hellboy rejected his demonic nature and fights for "the good guys" as a member of the BPRD (Bureau for Paranormal Research and Defense).

Besides being a great comic book, HELLBOY has also starred in two live-action and two animated movies.

Homo superior *(proper noun)*
In the X-Men comics, *Homo superior* represents the next stage of human evolution—the Mutants, many of whom have super powers.
HOMO SUPERIOR *refers to the Mutants of the Marvel Universe, not Elton John, although he would make a very cool superhero, especially during his 1970s period.*

The Hulk *(proper noun)*
A Marvel character created by Stan Lee and Jack Kirby in 1962 about a scientist named Bruce Banner, who, after being exposed to gamma rays, has the ability to transform into the giant green Hulk when he gets angry. *HULK smash!!!*

icon *(noun)*
An icon is a concept described by Scott McCloud in *Understanding Comics* that explains how an image varies from a symbolic to a realistic representation of something.
The more realistic an ICON, the faster we receive the message; the more symbolic the icon, the longer it takes to perceive the message.

iconoclast *(noun)*
One of Scott McCloud's "four tribes" of comics, described in his influential book *Making Comics*. An iconoclast is a truth-seeker who uses comics for personal or political expression.
Examples of ICONOCLASTS include Robert Crumb and Alan Moore.

infinite canvas *(noun)*
The concept that a webcomic has an unlimited space on a webpage with which to work. A viewer can scroll all over a webcomic's infinite canvas.
With an INFINITE CANVAS, there are no limits! The universe is ours! Ha Ha Ha!

infinite Earths *(noun)*

DC Comics produced the crossover event *Crisis on Infinite Earths* to clean up their continuity, which had become very confusing as a result of so many different dimensions, including Crime-Syndicate Earth-3, an anthropomorphic Earth-C with characters such as Captain Carrot and Little Cheese, and an Earth where Bruce Wayne's parents lived.

I am confused by the INFINITE EARTHS storyline no matter what dimension I am in.

Iron Man *(proper noun)*

Making his first appearance in 1963, Iron Man is really Tony Stark, a wealthy industrialist, engineer, and playboy, who wears a suit of armor that he originally was forced to create to escape from captivity.

The song "IRON MAN" by Black Sabbath is not about Tony Stark. It is about a man turned to metal while traveling through time, who sees the apocalypse, tries to warn people about it, and since he cannot be understood, grows angry and causes the desctruction himself.

Jack Kirby *(proper noun)*

Also known as the "King of Comics," he was the Marvel artist responsible for co-creating with Stan Lee many famous characters including Spider-man, the Fantastic Four, the X-Men, the Incredible Hulk, the Avengers, and Thor. Eventually, he became dissatisfied with Marvel and left for DC and created the *Fourth World* comics. His unique artistic style, however, remains a staple of Marvel characters.

JACK KIRBY worked in animation as well, including designing characters for Thundarr the Barbarian.

The Killing Joke *(proper noun)*

A graphic novel written by Alan Moore that is psychologically heavy in its approach to the relationship between Batman and the Joker.

THE KILLING JOKE *was an influence on Tim Burton's* Batman*, as well as Christopher Nolan's* The Dark Knight.

GEEK FACT

Even though *The Killing Joke* is often hailed by geeks and critics alike as one of the greatest comic book stories ever written, its author, Alan Moore, doesn't think much of it, having since said, "It's not saying anything very interesting"

3

kite-eating tree *(noun)*
A tree in the *Peanuts* comic strip that always eats Charlie Brown's kites.
Charlie Brown once bit the KITE-EATING TREE to get back his kite and got in trouble with the Environmental Protection Agency.

Krypto *(proper noun)*
Superman's dog from Krypton who has super powers, much like Streaky the Supercat, Comet the Superhorse, and Beppo the Supermonkey.
When KRYPTO marks a fire hydrant, the hydrant melts.

Liefield style *(noun)*
Comic artist Rob Liefield is known for disproportionate superheroes with little feet and costumes that have many little pouches. Rob Liefield is the creater of Cable and Deadpool.
After gaining weight and having my feet bound, I am beginning to look like a superhero in the LIEFIELD STYLE.

ligne clair *(noun)*
An art style made famous by Herge, the creator of *The Adventures of Tintin*, using clear outlines for the subjects in the panels. Every inch of the panel is given equal attention, and the background is very realistic, even if the characters are not.
Not only did Herge draw in LIGNE CLAIR to simplify the art, but he also simplified his stories.

Love Showdown *(proper noun)*
A 1994 story by *Archie Comics* that was the most publicized event in Archie history and dealt with whether Archie would choose Betty or Veronica.
Right after the LOVE SHOWDOWN, another special issue returned the three back to their status quo, undoing the previous events.

Marvel 1602 *(proper noun)*
An alternate reality series that shows what Marvel heroes and villains would be like if they had existed in the Elizabethan era.
> *What's in a name? A MARVEL 1602 by any other name would smell just as sweet!*

Marvel Comics *(proper noun)*
One of the two most prominent comic book publishers (the other being DC Comics). Marvel is distinct from DC in that all of its heroes exist in "real world" settings—New York, California, New Mexico, and even Canada. For years, Marvel also prided itself that its characters were more realistic, struggling with issues like paying the rent, alcohol and drug abuse, dating, and so on.
> *Make mine MARVEL!*

Marvel method *(proper noun)*
A method of creating comics where the artist creates the comic only using a short synopsis and has greater control over the plot. Used by Stan Lee and Jack Kirby to perfection.
> *The modern graphic novels* Marvels *and* Kingdom Come, *with art by Alex Ross, were produced using the MARVEL METHOD.*

Marvels *(proper noun)*
A series by Kurt Busiek and Alex Ross that tells the story of the Marvel superheroes from the very beginning. It is told from the perspective of an ordinary person, a photographer.
> *MARVELS is a great display of the painting skills of Alex Ross, who is known for his photorealistic, iconic portraits of superheroes.*

Maus *(proper noun)*
Pulitzer Prize–winning graphic novel by Art Spiegelman about the Holocaust, but with mice as Jews and cats as Germans.
> *There's nothing funny about MAUS, even if you're German.*

GEEK QUIZ

Batman's utility belt has an item for every situation, helped by the fact that Bruce Wayne is so wealthy and has access to whatever he can imagine. What is *not* an item that has been included in Batman's utility belt?

a. Batarang

b. Kryptonite ring

c. Bat goo gun

d. Bat stapler

Answer: d

3

---

micropayment *(noun)*

A program that allows a comic reader to pay small incremental amounts to view web comics. They allow web comic artists to profit from their work because the payments are smaller and a reader may be more inclined to pay.

Between the car and the mortgage and my MICROPAYMENT, I am just maxed out this month.

mint condition *(noun)*

The highest quality of a comic book, giving it the highest value on the market. A rare comic's value can be drastically reduced if it is not of good quality.

I would love nothing more than to own a MINT CONDITION Action Comics #1, which is the first appearance of Superman and worth $1.5 million.

Minutemen *(proper noun)*

In Alan Moore's graphic novel *Watchmen*, the Minutemen are a group of superheroes around in the early 1940s that preceded the Watchmen.

When it comes to conversational attention span, my girlfriend says I must be one of the MINUTEMEN.

Mister Mxyzptlk *(proper noun)*

A supervillain of Superman from the fifth dimension who appears as an imp with magical powers. He can only be defeated if he says his own name backwards.

I can't even pronounce MISTER MXYZPTLK forwards, let alone backwards.

GEEK FACT

Words that are easy to pronounce backwards:
a. Dog
b. Saw
c. Was
   *cheated on the last one ☺

Modern Age *(proper noun)*

The period of comics from the late 1980s to the present. Examples include *Watchmen* and *The Dark Knight Returns*. In the Modern Age, many comics began exploring darker themes, gaining a more adult audience.

During the MODERN AGE, the major comic companies grew significantly, in part due to big-screen adaptions.

motion lines *(noun)*

The lines in comics to show speed or action. They are used heavily in manga but also in comics in general. A moving background is created using motion lines. It is a key component of manga when a character is moving at super speeds to attack an opponent.

The more I drink, the blurrier the MOTION LINES seem to get.

mutagen *(noun)*

A chemical or physical substance that alters the genetic structure of a living thing. A mutagen was responsible for the transformation that created the Teenage Mutant Ninja Turtles.

That's right. MUTAGEN. And you just thought the Teenage Mutant Ninja Turtles ate their Wheaties.

GEEK FACT

What are other creatures that have been transformed by a mutagen?

Michael Jackson: From young black man to old white woman to undead.

Madonna: From slut from Detroit to older slut from Detroit with muscles to really old slut from Detroit with fake English accent.

George W. Bush: From alcoholic loser to two-term president/war criminal.

My wife: From sexy Brazilian to sexy Brazilian not interested in sleeping with me anymore to someone who looks at me in the morning and wants to throw up.

Jesus: From carpenter to Messiah to popular first name for Puerto Ricans.

Kirstie Alley: From hot Vulcan to hot bartender to fat embarassment.

Mutant Registration Act *(proper noun)*

A legislative bill in the Marvel Universe that requires mutants to register themselves with the government; seen as controversial.

There are equivalents to the MUTANT REGISTRATION ACT in Watchmen *and the movie* The Incredibles.

Mutants *(proper noun)*

1. The *Homo superior* species as seen in the *X-Men* comics and movies.
2. A dangerous gang that torments Gotham City in *The Dark Knight Returns*.

Where to find MUTANTS? Any computer science class at UC Berkeley.

mylar *(noun)*

A polyester film used to bag comics in order to protect them from environmental damage and aging effects.

Mickey Rourke appears to have MYLAR grafted to his skin.

necroplasm *(noun)*

The substance that makes up the comic character Spawn's outfit, made of material originating in hell that gives him special abilities.

Once the NECROPLASM runs out of energy, it sends the hellspawn back to hell forever.

No-Prize *(proper noun)*

An award given out by Marvel Comics to its readers since 1964 for pointing out continuity errors or explaining how an error can be explained. It is now given out for any work of merit for Marvel.

I don't want to win the NO-PRIZE—it's what I am used to getting.

one-shot *(noun)*

A comic book that is a standalone and not part of a series.

Dragonball *and* The Fist of North Star *started out as ONE-SHOTs.*

onomatopoeia *(noun)*

When a sound is described using words. Used profusely in comic books to portray sound effects, such as "Wham!" "Boooom!" "Kapwing!"

Does the word ONOMATOPOEIA sound like what it means?

panels *(noun)*

Used in comics to contain the pictures and put them in sequential order to tell a story. According to Scott McCloud in *Understanding Comics*, panels can be of different types, including picture specific, word specific, or a combination.

Chris Ware has brilliant PANEL design in his comics.

panel-to-panel transitions *(noun)*

Another Scott McCloud term from *Understanding Comics*, used to describe the different types of transitions between comic book panels. They are moment-to-moment, action-to-action, subject-to-subject, scene-to-scene, aspect-to-aspect, and non-sequitur transitions.

Understanding how PANEL-TO-PANEL TRANSITIONS operate will help any comic artist succeed.

pannapictagraphist *(noun)*

A person who collects comic books.

The first step of PANNAPICTAGRAPHISTS Anonymous is admitting you are powerless against the comic books.

Phantom Zone *(noun)*
A prison dimension in the Superman universe, previously home to super-villians like General Zod. The "locked door" of the Phantom Zone was portrayed in the first *Superman* movie as a mirror flying through outer space.
> *Yo, you know where you at, homie? You a long way from Starbucks. This is the PHANTOM ZONE!*

phasing *(noun)*
A superhero power that involves being able to pass through physical objects, like Shadowcat.
> *Don't PHASE me, bro.*

pictorial vocabulary *(noun)*
A concept introduced by comic theorist Scott McCloud in *Understanding Comics* that states that a picture in a comic is comprised of reality, language, and the picture plain.
> *The next time I read a comic, I will have to analyze it in terms of its PICTORIAL VOCABULARY.*

political cartoon *(noun)*
Typically contains two parts: a caricature of a public figure in grotesque manner, and an allusion to them in a certain situation.
> *The first POLITICAL CARTOON was by Ben Franklin with the words "Join or die" and a snake with severed parts representing colonies. Franklin worked tirelessly on the cartoon, making sure he was early to bed and early to rise.*

power cosmic *(noun)*
In Marvel Comics, the vast energy wielded by Galactus, Destroyer of Worlds. It is also what gives his herald, the Silver Surfer, his power.
> *Love is the POWER COSMIC.*

Power Ring *(noun)*
Used by the Green Lantern Corps. Creates a powerful green energy object in whatever form the wearer imagines.
> *The POWER RING is ineffective against the color yellow and therefore would be useless in a fight with a banana.*

GEEK FACT

In the 1983 movie *Breathless*, Richard Gere's character is obsessed with the Silver Surfer and reads the comics throughout the movie (sometimes out loud). Ladies, this movie is where geeks first discovered the pickup line, "Love is the power cosmic." Strangely, most geeks have much less success with the line than Richard Gere did.

Preacher *(proper noun)*
A controversial, violent, and brilliant comic book series written by Garth Ennis and drawn by Steve Dillon about a preacher named Jesse Custer, who, with the power of a supernatural creature named Genesis, can make anyone obey his commands. Also starring Cassidy the vampire; his gunwielding girlfriend, Tulip; Herr Starr; and the Saint of Killers.
PREACHER is one of the greatest comics ever and combines very offensive material with a very touching story.

prestige format *(noun)*
A type of comic that was originally printed by DC Comics that used higher-quality paper and a thicker cover.
PRESTIGE FORMAT originated with the printing of The Dark Knight Returns *in 1986.*

psionic blast *(noun)*
A superhero power that involves attacking another's mind and causing pain, unconsciousness, or even memory loss. Used by Psylocke, a mutant in the Marvel universe.
I was having a PSIONIC BLAST battle with my quiche.

Ratbert *(proper noun)*
A rat character in the comic strip *Dilbert* that is very naive and easy to manipulate.
To my father, everyone is a RATBERT.

RAW *(proper noun)*
A comic book anthology edited by Art Spiegelman and Francoise Mouly in the 1980s that collected the works of many famous artists such as Robert Crumb and Chris Ware.
Maus, the famous graphic novel, was first serialized in RAW.

recognition *(noun)*
The telepathic ability of elves in *Elfquest*, where they exchange soul names and then bond in a deep and sexual way.
RECOGNITION is involuntary and can cause conflict when someone already is in a relationship.

Rube Goldberg device *(noun)*
A type of device that is very complex and usually involves a chain of events that actually only performs a simple task. Appeared in comic strips by Reuben Goldberg, who eventually won a Pulitzer Prize.
In Pee-wee's Big Adventure, *a RUBE GOLDBERG DEVICE is used to make Pee-wee's breakfast.*

saddle stitch *(noun)*
The binding on a comic book.
The value of this Giant Size X-Men #1 *is not as high as it could be because the SADDLE STITCH is totally ruined.*

Sandman *(proper noun)*
A hugely successful comic book written by Neil Gaiman and published by the DC Comics imprint Vertigo. It was hailed by both readers and critics alike and won the World Fantasy Award in 1991 for Best Short Story.
Singer Tori Amos is a fan of SANDMAN.

The Savage Sword of Conan *(proper noun)*
A black and white comic book featuring the adventures of Robert E. Howard's Conan the Barbarian. First published in 1974 by Curtis Magazines (an imprint of Marvel Comics), it attracted the attention of some of the best artists in the industry because as a "magazine" it did not have to adhere to the standards of the Comics Code Authority nor shy away from the brutal violence and buxom wenches of Howard's stories. Not surprisingly, it was one of the most popular comic books of the 1970s.
When I was twelve, I couldn't buy Playboy, *but SAVAGE SWORD OF CONAN was almost as good.*

GEEK FACT

On the set of the movie, *Conan the Barbarian*, the special effects crew needed to mix the fake blood concentrate with water. But the water kept freezing because it was so cold. So instead they used vodka, which led to the actors swallowing the blood instead of spitting it out. Understandably, a lot of fake blood was consumed.

Scud *(proper noun)*

A disposable robot Heart Breaker Series 1373 assassin that can be bought from a vending machine that will self-destruct after killing the target. Also the title and main character in the *Scud* comic by Rob Schrab that keeps its target alive so that it will stay alive.

If we could really buy a disposable assassin like SCUD, would that put human assassins out of a job?

Secret Wars *(proper noun)*

A Marvel crossover in the '80s that involved a cosmic being called the Beyonder who transported heroes and villains to a battle world with advanced weaponry so that they could fight each other.

The SECRET WARS was also an excuse for a line of toys, as was the case with many things in the '80s.

Shazam *(phrase)*

Word used by Billy Batson to become Captain Marvel, created in 1939. It is also the name of the wizard that grants him his powers.

"SHAZAM! Well, gollee, surprise, surprise, surprise!" —Gomer Pyle

S.H.I.E.L.D *(proper noun)*

Short for Strategic Hazard Intervention Espionage Logistics Directorate, a covert military agency led by Nick Fury (as seen in the *Iron Man* movies).

S.H.I.E.L.D. will be a strong presence in all of the Marvel films.

Silver Age *(proper noun)*
The period of comic books from the mid 1950s to around 1970. Noted for an expansion in artistic styles and the time when superheroes came to dominate comic books. It is also the period when some of the most influential comic book creators rose to fame, such as Stan Lee, Jack Kirby, John Buscema, Jim Steranko, Denny O'Neill, Roy Thomas, Neal Adams, Barry Windsor-Smith, and John Romita Sr. Popular characters who first appeared in the Silver Age include Spider-Man, the Flash, the Hulk, and the Fantastic Four.
The SILVER AGE was a successful and expansive period in comics. It is also when horror and crime comics gained popularity.

slab *(verb)*
To place a comic book in a plastic case to protect it from damage.
I need to SLAB my Giant Size X-Men #1.

Sinister Six *(proper noun)*
A supervillain group that teamed up to fight Spider-Man. It consisted of Doctor Octopus, Vulture, Electro, Kraven, Mysterio, and Sandman. First appeared in 1964 and has always had a rotating cast.
Spoiler alert: Spider-Man always beats the SINISTER SIX in the end.

snikt *(noun)*
The sound that Marvel character Wolverine's claws make when they extend.
Before "Schwing!" there was SNIKT.

soul name *(noun)*
From the comic *Elfquest*, it is a name that is a secret known only to one's lover and reveals one's innermost identity.
No one knows, but Mike's SOUL NAME is Gertrude.

speech balloon *(noun)*
Used in comics to display dialogue, it is a white shape with an arrow or trail that originates from the character who is speaking.
The SPEECH BALLOON originates from the medieval phylactar, a label in the form of a scroll that stated characters or explanations. But you probably already knew that.

Spider-man *(proper noun)*

A Marvel superhero created in 1962, in reality the geeky Peter Parker, who was bitten by a radioactive spider and given special abilities including the ability to climb walls.

SPIDER-MAN's popularity can partly be attributed to the fact that his secret identity is that of a regular geeky high-school student, to whom many fans can relate.

splash page *(noun)*

A page in a comic book that is one image. It is usually page one of a comic book and includes the title and the creative team and many times, a dramatic image.

I couldn't afford the whole comic book, so I just bought the SPLASH PAGE.

Stan Lee *(proper noun)*

Born Stanley Martin Lieber, Stan Lee is arguably the single most influential comic book creator ever. During his stint at Marvel Comics, he cocreated Spider-Man, the Fantastic Four, the X-Men, the Avengers, Iron Man, the Hulk, Daredevil, and Doctor Strange and wrote many of the comic books.

STAN LEE is to comic books what Elvis and the Beatles are to rock 'n' roll.

Superman *(proper noun)*

Also known as the "Man of Steel," he is the famous superhero created in 1938 by Jerry Siegel and Joe Shuster. Originally born as Kal-El on the planet Krypton before its destruction, he was sent to Earth. There, he developed powers as a result of exposure to Earth's yellow sun, which made him "faster than a speeding bullet, more powerful than a locomotive, and able to leap tall buildings in a single bound."

The word "SUPERMAN," or Übermensch, was originally coined by Friedrich Nietzsche.

swipe *(verb)*

A term in comics meaning to take a panel from something else and use it again, such as using someone else's art as an outline for a new work but not crediting them.

Jack Kirby has been SWIPED many times, but supposedly he also swiped from Hal Foster, the creator of Prince Valiant.

symbiote *(noun)*
A parasitic alien life form that binds to a person and causes physical and mental changes in the host. Responsible for the supervillains Venom and Carnage.

> *In the comic books, Spidey's SYMBIOTE suit made him more aggressive and brutal. In the movie, it made him dance. Epic fail.*

Teenage Mutant Ninja Turtles *(proper noun)*
A crime-fighting group of four turtles who were transformed by mutagen and are experts in martial arts. Leonardo, the leader, wields katana blades, Donatello, the most intelligent one, uses a bo staff, Raphael, the hot head, uses the sai, and Michelangelo, the partier, uses nunchucks. They are led by Splinter, their giant rat sensei. They became hugely successful in comics, cartoons, movies, and toys.

> *The Shredder is the arch nemesis of the TEENAGE MUTANT NINJA TURTLES.*

telekinesis *(noun)*
The superpower in comics where a person can control objects with just his or her mind.

> *If you haven't tried using TELEKENESIS to grab the remote control from off the coffee table, then you aren't much of a geek.*

thagomizer *(noun)*
The tail spikes of a stegosaurus, invented by *Far Side* cartoonist Gary Larson in a comic where a caveman is lecturing on the thagomizer, which was named after Thag Simmons, and picked up by the scientific community.

> *A THAGOMIZER would destroy a* Strigiphilus garylarsoni.

The Tick *(proper noun)*
A superhero created by Ben Edlund in the mid-1980s, the Tick was a comic spoof on the superhero genre. It proved to be so popular that it was later made into a Saturday morning cartoon and a live-action TV series starring Patrick Warburton of *Seinfeld* fame. His battle cry is, "Spoon!"

> *"Wicked men, you face THE TICK!"*

Tintin *(proper noun)*

In the immensely popular graphic novels by Herge, a character who goes on many adventures with Captain Haddock and Snowy the dog. Soon to be a movie blockbuster by Steven Spielberg and Peter Jackson.

I was in a TINTIN-like adventure the other day when I found an ancient manuscript at a garage sale leading me to a hidden treasure in Borduria.

transmogrifier *(noun)*

A device created by Calvin of the comic strip *Calvin and Hobbes* by Bill Watterson. The transmogrifier (actually a cardboard box) can transform its user into any other form, including a duck, a pink owl, or a bug-eyed monster.

C'mon! Let's use the TRANSMOGRIFIER to change Dad into an ATM!

Triceratons *(proper noun)*

An aggressive alien race in the *Teenage Mutant Ninja Turtles* universe that first appeared in the original comic book series and resembles an anthropomorphic triceratops.

The TRICERATON Zog helps the turtles because he is crazy and thinks they are his superior officers.

two-ply *(noun)*

The 11" × 17" boards that comic book artists use to create the original artwork for a comic book.

If you are serious about becoming a comic book artist, you should use TWO-PLY.

Ultimate Nullifier *(proper noun)*

The most dangerous weapon ever, the weapon will completely destroy any target. Used by Reed Richards of the Fantastic Four against Galactus.

The ULTIMATE NULLIFIER is working in conjunction with Oxy-clean on a new treatment for acne.

Ultimates *(noun)*

A reimagining of Marvel's Avengers, created by Mark Millar, and set in Marvel's Ultimate Universe.

"Why is the ULTIMATE'S version of Nick Fury in Iron Man *based on Samuel L. Jackson?"*

"Say 'why' one more time, m*th#@ f8@&#@! Go on. I dare you."
"Oh. That's wh—"

Ultimate Universe *(noun)*
A reimagining of the Marvel Universe where the classic heroes and stories were updated for a modern audience. The first title, *Ultimate Spider-Man*, premiered in 2000 and was a huge hit. It was both criticized and praised for its "deconstructionist" storytelling.

> *The ULTIMATE UNIVERSE is also sometimes referred to as Marvel 1610.*

underground comix *(noun)*
Small press independent comics in the 1960s and 1970s that focused on sex and drugs and typically were psychedelic in nature.

> *If you are chronically disappointed that Wonder Woman never takes off her leotard or smokes peyote, go get the UNDERGROUND COMIX version.*

unstable molecules *(noun)*
A fictional technology in the Marvel Universe that allows superheroes to wear costumes that will stretch to any size, won't rip apart or burn, and can even turn the wearer invisible.

> *UNSTABLE MOLECULES keep Mr. Fantastic in costume when he stretches and keep She-Hulk's bra from bursting from the pressure.*

GEEK QUIZ

Comic books are increasingly becoming source material for movies, although some movies come from comic books that don't include popular or traditional superheroes. Which of the following movies is *not* based on a comic?

a. *A History of Violence*

b. *Hancock*

c. *Road to Perdition*

d. *Mystery Men*

Answer: b

Usagi Yojimbo *(proper noun)*

Rabbit bodyguard. A comic by Stan Sakai about an anthropomorphic feudal Japan and a ronin rabbit named Usagi. Influenced by the work of Akira Kurosawa and his movie *Yojimbo.*

If a tortoise and USAGI YOJIMBO raced, who would you bet on?

Vertigo *(proper noun)*

A DC Comics imprint that publishes comic books of a more adult nature, including such titles as *V for Vendetta*, *A History of Violence*, *Y: The Last Man*, and *Preacher*.

The VERTIGO characters rarely cross over into the regular DC universe.

Watchmen *(proper noun)*

A comic-book series created by Alan Moore and artist Dave Gibbons in 1986 that gives a much darker and more realistic take on superheroes, one that takes place in an alternate universe where superheroes have been outlawed. After one of the Watchmen, the Comedian, has been killed, the investigation into his death leads to the discovery of a diabolical plot. Alan Moore initially wanted to use characters already in existence for the series, but DC didn't want their characters to die or become dysfunctional, so Moore created new characters based on the ones he initially planned on using.

"Who watches the WATCHMEN?"

Weapon X *(proper noun)*

A project by the Canadian government to create super soldiers out of mutants, it is responsible for binding adamantium to Wolverine's skeleton. Sabretooth and Deadpool were also in Weapon X.

Canada? Really? LOL. ANY other country would be believable. HAITI would be a more believable location for WEAPON X than Canada.

webcomic *(noun)*

A self-published comic on the Internet. They are numerous, more experimental, and often well made, but rarely make any financial gains. Two of the most popular webcomics are *Penny Arcade* and *PVP (Player vs. Player).*

Penny Arcade is an example of a WEBCOMIC that is now popular in graphic novel form.

What If . . . ? *(proper noun)*
A series by Marvel Comics that told one-shot "what if" stories, such as "What if Spider-Man joined the Fantastic Four?" "What if the Punisher's family had not been killed?" and "What if Wolverine were lord of the vampires?"
WHAT IF Twilight *didn't suck?*

widescreen comics *(noun)*
Comics that are written like movies and cinematic in how they are presented. The word comes from Warren Ellis, a prominent comic book writer.
After WIDESCREEN COMICS comes state-of-the-art 3D comics that take years and millions of dollars to produce and then totally suck.

Will Eisner *(proper noun)*
An acclaimed and influential comic-book creator who created the comic hero The Spirit and is responsible for helping graphic novels become a legitimate art form. Each year, the Will Eisner Comic Industry Awards are given to outstanding comic creators.
For a proper introduction to the work of WILL EISNER, skip the movie The Spirit *and check out his graphic novels, such as* A Contract with God.

Chapter 4

GEEKS GO TO JAPAN: ANIME AND MANGA

As Japan has grown into a world economic power, second only to the United States, its culture also has grown in influence throughout the world. In particular, Japanese anime and manga have developed an international audience that includes millions of readers and viewers in the United States, Europe, and beyond.

Anime and manga also have influenced American comic books and movies. In comparison with classic American comic books, manga has a broader range, including the use of unconventional story lines, adult themes, and experimental storytelling methods. This influence can be seen in the work of Frank Miller, the *Power Puff Girls*, and *The Matrix*.

Afro Samurai *(proper noun)*

A manga featuring an African American hip-hop samurai.

> *The soundtrack for the* AFRO SAMURAI *anime was produced by Wu-Tang Clan member RZA.*

AMV *(noun)*

Short for anime music video. Seen in abundance on Youtube.com, where fans make music videos using clips from anime.

> *Please, no more AMVs using Nickelback songs.*

anime *(noun)*

Japanese animation that is usually more adult in nature and more complex than American cartoons.

> *ANIME has had a profound effect on Japanese culture.*

animegao *(noun)*

Also known as a doller. A person dressed in cosplay that is also wearing a facemask that is meant to look like an anime character.

> *An ANIMEGAO mask is much sexier than a paper bag.*

anime eyes *(noun)*

Large eyes, usually accompanied by a small mouth, as seen in manga and anime; many people in Japan have tried to imitate through plastic surgery.

> *In Singapore, ANIME EYES are considered mad chio (cute).*

GEEK FACT

In anime and manga, you may notice that the characters always have a wide variety of hair colors, whereas Japanese people have naturally dark hair. The reason this is done is to be able to easily differentiate the characters and still be able to draw them simply. This may have in turn led Japanese people to dye their hair to match anime characters.

aniparo *(noun)*

Anime parody. It is a type of anime that is a parody and usually uses a super deformed style.

> *Fans around the world create their own ANIPARO, and the quality is not always professional.*

baka *(noun)*
A common Japanese word often used in anime and manga that means "stupid."

So many Westerners now know the meaning of the word "BAKA" that the Japanese have been forced to use different words to insult us to our faces.

GEEK QUIZ

Manga is read by people of all ages in Japan and is a $4 billion industry. That is a lot of manga. On average, how long does it take a Japanese reader to read three hundred pages of a manga comic?

a. Twenty minutes

b. Thirty minutes

c. Forty minutes

d. One minute

Answer: a

Astro Boy *(proper noun)*
Created in 1952 by Osamu Tezuka as a manga, would later become the first anime in 1963. Astro Boy is a robot with black underpants and a pointy haircut who was adopted by Professor Ochanomizu and fights evil.

In 2009, an ASTRO BOY movie came out that was in 3D computer animation.

bishojo *(noun)*
A type of Japanese video game that features anime-style girls with game-play similar to a "Choose your own adventure" story but with romantic or erotic content.

Some otaku prefer BISHOJO to actually interacting with women.

bishounen *(noun)*
The anime and manga term for a "pretty boy" or a man with feminine looks.

The vampires and werewolves in Twilight *are BISHOUNEN.*

bosozoku *(noun)*

Japanese motorcycle gangs that modify their bikes, engage in reckless behavior, and dress in outfits such as colored jumpsuits. Portrayed in the manga and anime *Akira*.

Kaneda's BOSOZUKU gang fights against the clown motorcycle gang in Akira.

bunkoban *(noun)*

A manga book that is novel-sized and larger in length than a normal manga book.

Is that a BUNKOBAN in your pocket or are you just happy to see me?

catgirl *(noun)*

An anime or manga character that is a girl with cat ears and a tail, very popular among fans.

If you like Catwoman, you'll love CATGIRL.

chibi *(noun)*

A term in manga and anime for a little character or a childlike version of a character.

Mini-me is a CHIBI version of Dr. Evil.

Clamp *(proper noun)*

A famous all-female manga creation team that has worked together since the 1980s and has created works such as *Tsubasa: Reservoir Chronicle* and *Cardcaptor Sakura*.

CLAMP is a mysterious entity to its fans, making few public appearances.

compilation movie *(noun)*

An anime film that puts together footage from the television show, condensing a longer story line into the length of a short movie.

Ghost in the Shell: Stand Alone Complex *is an example of a COMPILATION MOVIE.*

Daidarabotchi *(proper noun)*

A huge nature spirit in Japanese myth that was also seen in the anime *Princess Mononoke* as the Night Walker.

The DAIDARABOTCHI once put Mount Fuji and Mount Tsukuba on a scale to weigh them.

dattebayo *(phrase)*
Naruto's catch phrase meaning "Believe it" in the English-dubbed anime, but has no real meaning in Japanese.
I have to go to the store and pick up some brocolli, DATTEBAYO!

Death Note *(proper noun)*
An anime, manga, and live-action movie about a demonic notebook that has the power to kill whoever's name is written within. The story centers around a game of cat and mouse between the owner of the notebook, Light, and the one tracking him down, L.
After seeing the movie DEATH NOTE, I threw out all my notebooks so my girlfriend couldn't kill me.

GEEK FACT

Geek Confessions
My father found a notebook in my great uncle's drawer. It was titled the "Death Book" and contained the birth dates and death dates of hundreds of celebrities and friends and family members. Next to all of our names—even the young ones like me—there was our name, our birth date, and our "death date" followed by a question mark. Creepy.

Doraemon *(proper noun)*
A manga character that is a time-travelling robotic cat, named the "anime ambassador" of Japan by the Foreign Ministry.
On an ambassadorial mission, there was an international incident when DORAEMON was placed on the menu at a Cantonese restaurant.

doujinshi *(noun)*
A manga that is a one-shot and usually published independently by an amateur.
DOUJINSHI is very popular in Japan, but in America it would be compared to pornographic fan fiction.

Dragon Ball *(noun)*
There are seven magical Dragon Balls. Once all are found, a dragon appears and grants a wish.
> *If I found all the DRAGON BALLS, I would wish for unlimited wishes.*

dub slang *(noun)*
When an anime is dubbed in English but slang words are added, such as "you trippin' " or "he so fine."
> *Unlike subtitles, DUB SLANG is off the chain, yo.*

Duel Monsters *(proper noun)*
The fictional card game in the manga and anime *Yu-Gi-Oh!* where players use cards to fight each other using monsters. The Yu-Gi-Oh! Trading Card Game is based on this game.
> *The actual Yu-Gi-Oh! Trading Card Game is not exactly like DUEL MONSTERS because the fictional game must serve the plot of the story.*

ecchi *(noun)*
Manga and anime that is sexual in nature, from pin-up girls to fanservice to breast groping.
> *Has my new ECCHI tentacle manga come in yet?*

educational manga *(noun)*
A type of manga for teaching, such as Falcon's Computer Hacking
> *EDUCATIONAL MANGA is about as entertaining as anything educational, which means its not.*

Espers *(noun)*
A powerful group of aging but childlike psychics who were the schoolmates of Akira, the deadly telepath from the manga and anime *Akira*.
> *The word "ESPERS" comes from the term ESP (extrasensory perception).*

Evangelion *(proper noun)*
Also known as Evas or EVA. The humanoid mechas in *Neon Genesis Evangelion* that are biologically integrated with the pilot.
> *The pilot of an EVANGELION must have his or her soul synchronized with the mecha, which causes the pilot and mecha to experience the same physical sensations, including pain.*

eyecatch *(noun)*
In anime, the screen that plays right before and right after commercial breaks and includes the name of the anime and sometimes interesting info about the characters or story.

The EYECATCH used for Pokemon *includes a guessing game to test whether the viewer can guess a Pokemon's name from its silhouette.*

face fault *(noun)*
A character's facial expression in anime and manga of exaggerated surprise or anger.

Even though it was an American production, the Teen Titans *cartoon had a very anime style and the characters displayed FACE FAULTs.*

fanservice *(noun)*
In an anime or manga, when there are elements of a sexual nature that are not relevant to the story.

Jeb only buys anime for the FANSERVICE breast shots.

fansub *(noun)*
An anime that has been translated and subtitled by fans. Copyright laws make it illegal to distribute fansubs in many countries, and it is therefore controversial.

FANSUBS can be intentionally or unintentionally humorous.

figure moe zoku *(noun)*
An otaku who is obsessed with their toy collection.

Andy from The 40-Year-Old Virgin *is a FIGURE MOE ZOKU.*

filler *(noun)*
Episodes in an anime that serve no purpose in the story line and are used to give the manga time to catch up with the anime, because the manga may take longer to produce.

My life is a FILLER, with no purpose or interesting storyline.

Geass *(proper noun)*
From the anime and manga *Code Geass*, a unique special power given to a human by an immortal that will grant the human immortality and the ability to pass on Geass to another. Also called the "Power of King."

Bob was offered GEASS, but after taking a good look at the world around him, passed it up.

genga cel *(noun)*
An original anime cell before it's been colored or edited.
> *Surprisingly, there is an active market for GENGA CEL art.*

ghost hack *(verb)*
To hack into a person's brain through their cybernetic implants or cyber-brains and disrupt their reality, sometimes forcing them to perform crimes such as assassination, as seen in *Ghost in the Shell*.
> *GHOST HACKING is a desired quality for a robosexual.*

Goku *(proper noun)*
The main character in the anime and manga, *Dragonball*, who begins as a child from another planet and eventually becomes an adult with powerful abilities such as emitting energy blasts, as seen in the series *Dragonball Z*.
> *GOKU's alien tail was cut off many times before finally being permanently removed.*

Gundam *(noun)*
A mobile suit, the most famous of which is the RX-78-2 Gundam, used by the Earth Federation to fight the Principality of Zeon.
> *Do you have a GUNDAM suit in a 42 regular?*

harem *(noun)*
A genre in manga and anime where a single male character is surrounded by multiple females and sexual situations and drama ensues.
> *Ah, the HAREM genre of manga; reminds me of when I was in college.*

hentai *(noun)*
Anime or manga that is pornographic in nature.
> *I wonder why my college roommate, Alex, was so into HENTAI?*

hokuto shinken *(noun)*
A martial art used by Kenshiro, star of the anime and manga *The Fist of North Star*, that allows the user to harness energy and touch certain pressure points, causing the victim to explode, be split in half, or something else equally disgusting.
> *The average person uses 30 percent of his or her body strength, while someone trained in HOKUTO SHINKEN uses 100 percent.*

GEEKTIONARY

hunter-warrior *(noun)*
Bounty hunters in the manga and anime *Battle Angel Alita* that also serve as law enforcers due to the lack of police.
Dog the Bounty Hunter would not last a second against a HUNTER-WARRIOR.

itasha *(noun)*
Cars that are painted with anime or video game characters who are mostly girls.
Have you ever seen an ITASHA do a Tokyo drift?

jutsu *(noun)*
A supernatural technique, skill, or trick used by the ninja in *Naruto* by harnessing chakra, which is a ninja's basic energy source.
Examples of JUTSU are a fire ball and creation of a shadow clone.

Kamehameha *(proper noun)*
An energy attack emanating from the hands used mainly by Goku in *DragonBall*.
Goku uses a double KAMEHAMEHA against Piccolo.

kawaii *(adjective)*
Sometimes called super kawaii. In Japanese, *kawaii* means "cute." Emphasizes very girly childlike themes such as ornately ruffled dresses, cartoon characters, and commercial logos, plus stuffed animals and toys.
The KAWAII cuteness in Japanese cartoons sometimes makes me want to hurl.

kemonomimi *(noun)*
A concept in manga/anime where the people, usually girls, have animal-like features such as cat ears.
KEMONOMIMI . . . Japan's answer to the furries.

Kyuubi *(proper noun)*
The nine-tailed demon fox that is sealed within Naruto, who draws upon its power. Once enough power is drawn from the fox, it will be released from Naruto.
KYUUBI and Naruto are in constant battle for power.

light novel *(noun)*
Japanese novels that are written for junior-high and high-school students that are less serious than conventional novels and usually include numerous illustrations. Light novels are often adapted in animes and mangas.
LIGHT NOVEL publishers are always looking for new talent and receive thousands of submissions each year.

lolicon *(noun)*
A genre in manga that depicts girls, usually childlike, in an erotic manner.
LOLICON is bizarre and perverted and therefore prevalent on 4chan.

love pillow *(noun)*
A large pillow from Japan with a picture of a sexy anime girl printed on it that is used as a sex toy. The girl's version is a "boyfriend pillow" that includes two "arms" to hold the girl.
Forget the LOVE PILLOW, what's the Japanese word for "straightjacket?"

mahou shoujo *(noun)*
A genre in anime focusing on magical girls with special abilities who fight evil, such as *Sailor Moon*.
If Claire were a MAHOU SHOUJO, she would be Sailor Mercury because they both share a love of knowledge.

maid café *(noun)*
Cafés in Japan where the waitresses dress as maids or other outfits for fans of anime and manga.
MAID CAFÉ is another example of the brilliant and perverted nature of the Japanese mind.

manga *(noun)*
Comic books produced in Japan that read from right to left. Manga has revolutionized the comic book industry because of its dynamic techniques and adult-themed storylines.
The word MANGA is literally translated as "whimsical pictures."

mangaka *(noun)*
The artist or writer of a manga.
Now that I have drawn this short manga comic, instead of calling me Cecily, you have to refer to me as MANGAKA.

maniakku *(noun)*

A know-it-all obsessed with anime or manga.

Sayo is such a MANIAKKU she never stops talking about Naruto and always shows us clips from the show.

mecha *(noun)*

Giant mechanical vehicles or robots controlled by a human pilot. Very popular in anime and manga. Seen in *Robotech, Evangelion*, and the movie *Avatar*.

I need a navigator for the MECHA I created from thousands of tinker toys; so who is with me?

GEEK QUIZ

Did you notice that Goku used to have a monkey-like tail? The reason is because he is an alien. Goku from the anime and manga *Dragon Ball* is an extraterrestrial species named what?

a. Betazoid

b. Saiyan

c. Ocampa

d. Bakkataru

Answer: b

---

mecha musume *(noun)*

A term in manga and anime for girls wearing mech equipment or other types of hardware.

The anime Strike Witches *features MECHA MUSUME girls using mechanical devices on their legs to grant them special powers such as flight and super strength.*

meganekko *(noun)*

An anime or manga character that wears glasses.

MEGANEKKO is from two Japanese words and translates as "glasses girl."

moe *(noun)*
A Japanese term for someone who has an interest or even an attraction to a manga or anime character or type of character. Can also refer to a young female anime/manga character.

> *John never had a MOE-like attraction to anime girls. He saw himself as more of a robosexual.*

Moonie *(noun)*
A fan of *Sailor Moon*.

> *Sophia, look at your* Sailor Moon *collection. You are such a MOONIE!*

Naruto *(proper noun)*
Title character of a popular anime and manga about a boy ninja who has a nine-tailed demon-fox spirit within him giving him special abilities but also making him sometimes more violent and aggressive. Naruto has also spawned light novels, video games, and a trading card game.

> *NARUTO aspires to be a powerful ninja . . . don't we all?*

Neo-Tokyo *(proper noun)*
Tokyo of the future, usually after an apocalypse, that is the setting for many manga and anime, including *Akira*.

> *NEO-TOKYO was built after the destruction of Tokyo and is now filled with terrorists and gangs.*

nouvelle manga *(noun)*
An art movement that combines the elements of manga and Franco-Belgian art.

> *I don't want to hang out with Pierre at the café with his snobby NOUVELLE MANGA friends.*

Oh Dae-su *(proper noun)*
The main character in the manga and movie *Oldboy*, who was imprisoned for many years without knowing his crime before being suddenly released to chase down his captor.

> *Spolier Alert: OH DAE-SU probably wishes he was never released from his prison given what happened later.*

GEEK QUIZ

Never get a tattoo in another language unless you make sure you know what it means. What does your favorite anime character's name mean? The word "naruto," from the main character in the manga and anime *Naruto*, is translated as:

a. Storm ninja

b. Fox ninja

c. Anxious boy

d. Japanese fish cake

Answer: d

Oiroke *(proper noun)*
The technique created by anime and manga character Naruto that is based on sexiness and his ability into transform into a naked girl.
If men had the transformative ability of OIROKE, most would be in the women's locker room half the day.

omake *(noun)*
Special features on an anime DVD, including deleted scenes, documentaries, bloopers, and sometimes special comedy scenes.
A DVD without OMAKE is like sushi without raw fish.

One Piece *(proper noun)*
One Piece is a very popular manga and anime about a boy named Monkey D. Luffy who wants to impress his hero, the pirate Red-Haired Shanks, and find the legendary treasure, known as "One Piece" and become the Pirate King. Because he ate the Devil's Fruit, Monkey becomes deadweight in water, but he is able to stretch and inflate his body.
When the ONE PIECE treasure is found, supposedly "a grand battle that engulfs the entire world" will commence.

otaku *(noun)*
A fan with an obsession, often unhealthy, for manga, anime, or video games.
I am a Spam OTAKU. Got a problem with that?

OVA *(noun)*
Short for original video animation. Anime made for the direct-to-video market.
> *OVAs gained popularity in the VHS format during the 1980s anime boom.*

4

Panzer Kunst *(proper noun)*
A martial-arts style used by cyborgs, as seen in *Battle Angel Alita*.
> *After a PANZER KUNST battle, don't call an ambulance, call Radio Shack.*

Puppet Master *(proper noun)*
An artificial intelligence that can hack into and manipulate the minds of others, as seen in *The Ghost in the Shell*.
> *Geppetto and Buffalo Bob were the OGs of PUPPET MASTERs.*

Racer X *(proper noun)*
A masked racer in *Speed Racer*, revealed to be Rex Racer, the older brother of Speed Racer who anonymously helps out Speed on the racetrack.
> *RACER X is the brother who everyone thought died? What is this— a soap opera?*

Rock *(proper noun)*
A recurring manga and anime character created by Osamu Tezuka, seen in around sixty mangas and anime, including *Astro Boy* and *Metropolis*. Rock is defined by his black hair and dark sunglasses.
> *ROCK is not to be confused with "The Rock."*

Ryuk *(proper noun)*
A Shinigami in *Death Note* of frightening appearance that is responsible for the death note coming into the hands of Light Yugami, who is chased by world renowned detective, L.
> *RYUK is addicted to apples and suffers withdrawal without them.*

scanlation *(noun)*
Scanning a manga and placing it on the Internet with a translation.
> *Team, we need to complete all the SCANLATIONS before being bombarded with hate mail from angry otaku.*

scenery porn *(noun)*
Used in anime for scenery that is high in quality and displayed in long-lasting shots.
My mom found my stash of Home and Garden *under my bed. Now she knows I'm into SCENERY PORN.*

seiyuu *(noun)*
An anime voice actor.
Kikuko Inoue is a famous SEIYUU, known for her voice acting in Gundam, Ranma ½, Sailor Moon, *and dozens of other anime.*

settei sheet *(noun)*
Anime Studios use these sheets as a guide to draw the anime in the same style as the manga.
SETTEI SHEET is the anime equivalent of a model sheet.

Shinigami *(proper noun)*
As seen in the manga and anime *Death Note*, they are Death Gods that kill humans to prolong their lives; they are the originators of the titular death note.
The personification of death, the SHINIGAMI was brought from Europe to Japan in the nineteenth century.

shinobi *(noun)*
A ninja, or ninja in training, in *Naruto*. *Shinobi* is also a Sega game series that was first introduced as an arcade game in 1987.
The SHINOBI in Naruto *have special abilities such as mind control and generating lightning.*

shipping *(noun)*
A practice among fans of anime and manga who passionately desire and lobby for two characters to become romantically involved.
SHIPPING was extensive during The X-Files *run, when fans desperately wanted Mulder and Scully to hook up.*

Soul Reaper *(proper noun)*
From the anime and manga *Bleach*. Soul Reapers are members of a military group that brings souls to the afterlife. They fight against Hollows, who are uncooperative souls.
The job market for SOUL REAPERS has suffered in this recession.

4

sukeban (noun)
Dangerous and troublesome Japanese schoolgirl gangs with dyed hair and modified school girl outfits, sometimes potrayed in manga and anime.

Don't mess with the SUKEBAN, or they will make you pay for enjoying that hentai comic.

GEEK QUIZ

What is the name of the Japanese anime that was re-edited for American audiences and turned into *Voltron: Defender of the Universe* using new plots and dialogue?

a. *Voltage: Electric Wars*

b. *Beast King GoLion*

c. *Lion Tetsuo*

d. *Super Happy Robot Hour*

Answer: b

---

super deformed (noun)
A style of manga where the characters have small, fat bodies and over-sized heads.

Examples of SUPER DEFORMED IRL are Jay Leno, and Sloth from The Goonies.

superflat (noun)
An art movement originating with Takashi Murakami using manga and anime art styles that are flattened to send a message of shallow consumer culture.

SUPERFLAT was specifically created for the Western market.

super robot (noun)
A genre in anime and manga involving giant mechas that are usually controlled by pilots. Originated from *Tetsujin 28-go* (*Gigantor*), which was a 1950s manga.

All normal robots wish they could be a SUPER ROBOT.

tankobon *(noun)*
An umbrella term in manga for a book format that is the equivalent of a graphic novel.

Ranma ½ was collected into thirty-eight TANKOBON books with ten chapters each.

GEEK QUIZ
What is the name of the best selling manga of all time?
a. *One Piece*
b. *Slam Dunk*
c. *Naruto*
d. *Dragon Ball*

Answer: a

Unico *(proper noun)*
A manga and anime character that is a small unicorn created by the famous Osamu Tezuka, who also created Astro Boy.

UNICO has the power to make people happy, just like money.

yandere *(noun)*
A term that applies to manga and anime meaning someone who is nice at first before becoming violent and angry. Appeared in *Mobile Suit Gundam* and has been criticized for its use in *School Days* and *When They Cry*.

A real YANDERE, the first time I met my ex-stepfather he gave me an Eskimo Pie. The second time, he convinced my mother to force-feed me fatty pot roast until I vomited.

yuri *(noun)*
A genre in manga involving a sexual relationship between two women.

Ok, well, I understand YURI. See, that's a NORMAL fantasy—girl on girl action, not guy on girl robot action. And no tentacles.

Chapter 5

GEEKS IN CYBERSPACE: SCIENCE AND COMPUTERS

Science and computers were the original geeks' natural habitat. Such alpha geeks as Bill Gates, Steve Wozniak, and Stephen Hawking emerged from the worlds of science and technology. Using slide rules, geeks sent us into both space and cyberspace. Now, with the advent of social-networking Internet sites such as Facebook and the use of hand-held devices such as the iPhone, a geek-like obsession with technology and devices is entering into the mainstream. So, where better to learn about geekdom than from exploring science and computers?

10,000-hour rule *(noun)*

Theory by Malcom Gladwell, author of *Outliers*, that it takes 10,000 hours to become skillful at any task.

Bill Gates satisfied the 10,000-HOUR RULE on programming when he was given access to a computer as a thirteen-year-old.

2600

The 2600 Hz frequency is famous for allowing users to make free long-distance phone calls. The tone was originally discovered by a blind seven-year-old, Joe Engressia, who had whistled it into a phone. In the 1960s, Cap'n Crunch included a whistle in their cereal boxes that created the 2600 Hz tone and, as a result, the whistle was heavily used for phreaking.

There is a famous and useful magazine called 2600: The Hacker Quarterly.

3D modeling *(noun)*

The process of creating a 3D image with a computer using software such as Maya.

Hey, I work for a 3D MODELING agency, and I think you'd be perfect.

4chan *(proper noun)*

A website with image and message boards that is known for posting pictures of anime and manga and is responsible for many memes, such as the LOLCats and rickrolling, and has been criticized for its controversial content.

A member of 4CHAN was responsible for hacking into Sarah Palin's Yahoo account.

anaglyph image *(noun)*

An image meant to be seen using 3D glasses comprised of two colors, red and cyan, superimposed on each other and blurry until the glasses are used.

The longer you stare at an ANAGLYPH IMAGE without the special glasses, the sicker you get.

antikythera mechanism *(noun)*
A mechanical computer built around 100 B.C. that was used to describe the positions of celestial bodies and determine the appropriate time to commence the Olympic Games.

The ANTIKYTHERA MECHANISM was the precursor to the Macintosh Classic.

Arecibo message *(noun)*
A pictorial message sent from Earth into space for other life forms to receive, developed with the help of Carl Sagan, to show our knowledge of math and science and who we are. The message contains the numbers 1 through 10, the atomic numbers of the elements, and information about DNA, human physical characteristics and the solar system. It will take 25,000 years for the message to reach it's destination.

When the aliens receive our ARECIBO MESSAGE, they will laugh their asses off.

A/S/L *(noun)*
Short for age/sex/location. The pickup line in style when America Online was popular.

Ah, those were the glory days of the Internet. All it took was to say A/S/L and it was all downhill from there.

attwaction *(noun)*
When a person has a crush on someone they know only through Twitter.

I have a strong ATTWACTION to a girl I know on Twitter. Unfortunately, she lives in Russia.

augmented reality *(noun)*
Augmented reality combines real world and computer-generated data, where computer graphics are blended with real-world images in real time. The first-down line that is graphically overlaid on a football field during a live broadcast demonstrates the use of augmented reality. In a first-person shooter video game, the life bar and ammo overlaid on your screen are additional examples of augmented reality.

The Terminator sees that the probability of kicking your ass is 100% in an AUGMENTED REALITY diagnostic.

5.

avatar *(noun)*
An image or character that represents a user or player in a video game or online.
> *Watch out for old men using little school-girl AVATARS.*

backdoor *(noun)*
A weakness in a computer program that may be purposely or accidentally created by the maker that allows an outsider access to a computer system.
> *In the movie* WarGames *(a 1983 film that inspired a generation of computer geeks), Matthew Broderick's character hacks into NORAD's computers by figuring out the program's BACKDOOR.*

binary *(noun)*
A numerical system using only two numbers, 0 and 1. Also known as a base-2 system.
> *My dad taught me BINARY on the way to school in kindergarten and I was rewarded with donuts.*

GEEK QUIZ

What was the backdoor password in the movie *WarGames*?

a. Antikythera (a mechanical computer built around 100 B.C.)

b. Ylla Ydeehs (Ally Sheedy, the film's costar, spelled backwards)

c. Joshua (the name of the software designer's son)

d. Ripley (the name of Sigourney Weaver's character in *Alien*)

Answer: c

---

biohacker *(noun)*
A genetic engineer who experiments in DNA and genetics in an attempt to understand, change, or create something biological in nature, just as a computer hacker might try and break into a system to understand or alter it.
> *Doctor Victor Frankenstein was the original BIOHACKER.*

Black Swan *(proper noun)*
A theory created by Dr. Nassim Taleb about unpredictable events in history that have unexpectedly changed the world but that are often explained in retrospect as if they were foreseeable. The very rare black-colored swan is a metaphor for a very rare, random, and unpredictable event.

Taleb describes the success of the Internet and personal computers as BLACK SWANs.

bloop *(noun)*
A powerful and low-frequency underwater sound detected in the Pacific Ocean. Its source is unknown, but scientists have speculated that it is probably biological in origin. The sea creature making the sound would be much larger than any whale and could be an enormous sea monster.

I was scared to go in the ocean for fear of being impaled by a sting ray. After hearing about the BLOOP, I have to now worry about a prehistoric beast?

GEEK QUIZ

What is the largest sea creature?

a. Blue whale

b. Sperm whale

c. The Great Old One

Answer: c

blue box *(noun)*
A device used by hackers to access public telephones for free by recreating the tones used by operators to switch calls. They were built by phreaks from the 1960s to the 1980s.

The BLUE BOX got its name because the first one confiscated was in a blue case.

Boolean logic *(proper noun)*
George Boole was a nineteenth century English mathematician who developed Boolean logic, which is based upon a binary approach using only two states (Yes/no, true/false, on/off, 0/1). All computers are based on this Boolean binary system because the system mimics positive and negative electrical charges.

This is dialectics. It's very simple BOOLEAN LOGIC. You can't go out into space with fractions. What are you going to land on, one-quarter?

boobiecons *(noun)*
Emoticons that represent boobs. (.)(.)
Ha ha. He said BOOBIECONS, LOL.

brext *(verb)*
To break up with a significant other using a phone text.
My girlfriend BREXTED me with "C U never bye"

celebritweet *(noun)*
Twitters from celebrities or celebrities who Twitter.
Ashton Kutcher is the ultimate CELEBRITWEET. If it makes you feel better, he's a moron.

clustergeeking *(noun)*
Working on computer science homework way too much.
I've been CLUSTERGEEKING all night trying to debug this program.

computer widow *(noun)*
A person who is in a relationship with someone who spends all his time on the Internet or playing video or computer games.
I won't judge a man for creating a COMPUTER WIDOW until I have met his wife.

crack, cracking *(verb, adjective, noun)*
To get past software security features.
Mark always CRACKS software, he never pays for it. But the joke's on him because the CRACKING software always contains computer viruses.

code monkey *(noun)*
A professional computer programmer or someone who is a grunt and performs busy-work coding.
Get in your cage and back to work, you stupid little CODE MONKEY.

cross post *(verb)*
To post messages or news in many different places on the Internet at the same time.
The Internet is one big CROSS POST nowadays.

cybershooting *(noun)*
A so-called sport using remotely controlled robots over the Internet to hunt and shoot game animals.
Ever since his infamous hunting accident, former vice president Dick Cheney has stuck to CYBERSHOOTING.

deep web *(noun)*
Websites and files not readily available to the public and hidden from search engines.
The DEEP WEB is used by shape-shifting lizards to control society.

DRM *(noun)*
Short for digital rights management. Copyright-protection technology used in games and other copyrighted software to prevent piracy.
DRM is controversial because it may be too limiting, and it hurts the online pirating community—which includes just about everyone.

ego-surfing *(noun)*
The act of searching the Internet for one's own name.
I was EGO-SURFING today and found my name! Unfortunately, the Internet says I'm a tool.

emoticons *(noun)*
Characters on a keyboard or phone pad used to make a face or other image. :-)
EMOTICONS used to be reserved for women. Now, all my friends respond to my messages with smiley faces. What is the world coming to?

Flash *(proper noun)*

A programming language used in online videos and for animation, such as in webcomics and online games.

FLASH uses a small amount of bandwidth and takes less time to load due to the small file sizes.

Frankenfood *(noun)*

Food that comes from genetically altered plants and animals, in reference to *Frankenstein*.

My FRANKENFOOD is alive. It's a-l-i-v-e!

gematria *(noun)*

The process of applying numbers to words and trying to find a pattern.

Gematria is used in the movie Pi, *where Max uses his supercomputer, Euclid, to analyze patterns in the Torah.*

Googlewhacking *(noun)*

A popular activity that involves trying to find a Google search item that ends in only one result.

We tried GOOGLEWHACKING Geektionary and only 19,200 results came up. Whack!

grid computing *(noun)*

The accessing and use of multiple systems and computers for a common goal.

Projects involving the future of the Internet usually involve GRID COMPUTING with lightning-fast connections.

hackathon *(noun)*

When multiple programmers get together to complete one particular goal, such as hacking into the CIA's main computers and disseminating top-secret information on the Internet.

A HACKATHON is like a binge-drinking party for geeks—only without the drinking. It can still get you arrested though.

holography *(noun)*
A technique for recording and reconstructing waves emanating from an illuminated object. It is formed using two lasers, a reference beam and an illuminating beam, that combine to form an interference pattern. The final product has two images: a virtual one and a real one.

HOLOGRAPHY is a staple of science fiction, seen in the alien chess game in Star Wars *and in the device that creates a hologram of the user in* Total Recall.

hotspot *(noun)*
The radius from which a wireless Internet connection, if not protected, can be accessed by a nonsubscriber.

Some girl is sitting on the ground outside my apartment with her laptop trying to leech off my HOTSPOT.

identity tourism *(noun)*
When a computer user assumes an identity other than his or her own in a chatroom or MUD, such as a male pretending to be female or someone assuming another racial identity out of curiosity.

Because of rampant IDENTITY TOURISM, one must always be alert on social networking sites because the hot eighteen-year-old woman may actually be a fat sixty-year-old man sitting in his mother's basement.

infosnacking *(verb)*
To be on a work computer but not doing anything work related.

If you are tired of INFOSNACKING, steer clear of Reddit.com, Wikipedia.org, and LookAtTheseNakedPeopleInsteadOfWorking. net.

IRL *(noun)*
Online slang for "in real life."

Online, I am a witty, personable, successful person. IRL, I have no life, so I'm online all the time..

juice a brick *(verb phrase)*
To power up any electronic gadget, from a computer to a video camera.

Yo, JUICE THAT BRICK, son. I needs to get my geek on, dawg.

junk sleep *(noun)*
To fall asleep while connected to any technology, such as a computer or an iPod.

> *Last I remember, I was on track 14 and now I'm on track 790. That's some serious JUNK SLEEP!*

keyboard jockey *(noun)*
A derogatory term for an Internet user who makes claims or statements that cannot be backed up in real life.

> *Anyone who has the balls to join me on this quest, step forward. As for the rest of you KEYBOARD JOCKEYS, you can just hide behind your monitors and let us real men handle this.*

Leetspeak *(noun)*
Language used on the Internet that often uses ASCII characters or technical jargon to replace English letters or words.

> *"Hacker" in LEETSPEAK is haxor.*

LHC *(proper noun)*
Short for Large Hadron Collider. The largest and highest-energy particle accelerator in the world. It will cause the apocalypse in 2012 by generating an artificial black hole that will destroy the Earth.

> *If you really believe in the LHC apocalypse, you might be smoking too much THC!*

LRAD *(noun)*
Short for Long Range Acoustic Device. A powerful wave ray that inflicts severe pain on its target. Used by the Army in the Middle East and against modern pirates. It is rumored to have been used against the Hulk on several occasions, although the government denies any knowledge of such a creature.

> *LRAD appears to also be used by teenagers when they play Miley Cyrus music.*

meme *(noun)*
An idea or concept that is transferred from person to person.

> *The LOLcats MEME is more infectious than the common cold.*

microblogging *(noun)*
Blogging in short form, as seen in Twitter and Facebook updates.

As Marshall McLuhan said, "The book has become the blurb." Then the blurb became the blog, and now blogging has become MICROBLOGGING. Soon, grunting will be the most popular form of communication.

middle school dance *(noun)*
When in a video game, two players sit idly by while waiting for the other to establish a connection.

My friend won't initiate this P2P connection. Should I initiate? I don't know. What is this, a MIDDLE SCHOOL DANCE?

modeling *(noun)*
The process of studying and learning from an individual by copying his or her behaviors and possibly integrating them into your own repertoire.

The talented Mr. Ripley was an expert in MODELING and then emulating the behavior of others, such as Dickie Greenleaf.

mouselexic *(adjective)*
When an individual cannot capably or does not know how to use a mouse.

Look at him use the mouse. He's obviously MOUSELEXIC.

nanometer *(noun)*
A metric system unit of length equal to one-billionth of a meter.

The symbol for a NANOMETER is nm.

nanotechnology *(noun)*
The study of controlling matter and creating devices sized between 1 to 100 nanometers; in other words, materials and structures that operate on an atomic or molecular scale, such as carbon nanotubes. While nanotechnology has ambitious, long-term goals in medicine, genetics, and electronics, applications so far are more prosaic, such as in sunscreen, cosmetics, and household products. Nanotechnology is common in science fiction—for example Michael Crichton's *Prey*.

Check out my new nanotechnology water-proof pants!

NLP *(noun)*

Short for neuro-linguistic programming; the study of the words people use and how it reflects their subconscious perceptions of reality. A common application is using your words and thoughts to help lead you down a positive and successful path in life.

One NLP technique as seen in advertising is to anchor positive thoughts to a product.

observer effect *(noun)*

A concept in physics that states that if one observes a phenomenon, it will have an effect and change what is being observed.

A good way to test the OBSERVER EFFECT is to leer into your neighbor's bedroom. Make sure to not get caught or else you are no longer doing an experiment. You're just being a pervert.

paradox *(noun)*

A contradictory statement or occurrence.

Examples of a PARADOX are "This statement is false," "My dog is a cat," and "This book is good."

phishing *(noun)*

The illegal practice of acquiring sensitive user information, such as passwords or credit card information, while appearing to be a legitimate and trusted source.

I know this sounds like a PHISHING scheme, but we have this Nigerian friend, and if you send him your credit card number . . .

pornado *(noun)*

An occurrence, while looking at online porn, where an endless stream of porn popups bombard the computer screen.

A tornado is a devastating example of nature's fury, whereas a PORNADO is the direct result of you being a pervert.

render *(verb)*

To take the final step in generating CGI, taking the 3D model and turning it into a finished product.

Before he could RENDER his short computer-animated film, advances in animation rendered his movie obsolete.

render farm *(noun)*
A group of interconnected computers used to render CGI.
The man waited for the final texturization of the CGI animal's fur in the RENDER FARM . . . again.

reverse engineer *(verb)*
To determine the function and process of a device or system by examining only the end product. There is a famous incident where the Chinese tried to reverse engineer an American airplane but failed to take material type and weight into consideration. Epic Fail.
God should REVERSE ENGINEER my ex to find what went wrong with her.

robosexual *(noun)*
A person that has an attraction to robots or android girls.
The movie Blade Runner *spawned an entire generation of ROBOSEXUALS.*

RT *(verb)*
To retweet. To copy and send out someone else's tweet.
As Gandhi once said, to RT is the sincerest flattery.

screenager *(noun)*
A teenager who spends too much time in front of a computer screen.
I recently met a SCREENAGER on the Internet. Guess that's where they hang out. Who knew?

Second Life *(proper noun)*
A virtual world on the Internet that allows users to walk around, talk to others, and buy and sell goods.
The more developed your SECOND LIFE is, the less developed your first life is.

SETI *(proper noun)*
Short for Search for Extraterrestrial Intelligence. Any activity that involves the search for life outside of Earth.
I performed a cross-country SETI, but the only strange creatures I found were Texans.

sexting (noun)

Texting that involves setting up a sexual encounter or a discussion of sexual acts.

Me and my girlfriend were SEXTING each other all night even though we were in the same room.

Schrödinger's cat (noun)

A thought experiment where a cat is placed in a sealed box wherein a "diabolical mechanism" has been placed that couples the cat's life or death with the state of a subatomic particle that also is within the box. As long as the box remains sealed, we can neither observe the state of the subatomic particle nor know whether the cat is alive or dead. According to an interpretation of quantum physics, an unobservable or nonmeasurable subatomic particle does not occupy a definite state, just statistical probabilities of all possible quantum states, until the exact moment of quantum measurement, at which point all the probabilities collapse into a definite state. Thus, according to quantum theory, because the particle will not occupy a definite state until such time as the box is opened, then until such opening of the box, the cat must be both alive and dead, at least to the universe outside the box.

One nonintuitive finding of quantum physics, best shown by SCHRÖDINGER'S CAT, is that prior to observation, quantum objects have no precise location, only statistical probabilities of location.

GEEK QUIZ

What now-successful company did Ron Wayne cofound but unfortunately sell his shares in for only $2,300 early on, which would have been worth $22 billion in 2010?

a. Microsoft

b. Apple

c. Oracle

d. BMG Music

Answer: b

GEEKTIONARY

signal-to-noise ratio *(noun)*
A term used in analyzing sound to determine how the level of a signal is affected by random background noise, also used to describe the ratio of useful information in a webpage in comparison to false or irrelevant information.

The SIGNAL-TO-NOISE RATIO is out of control on the Internet.

simulacrum *(noun)*
Latin for "similarity"; a copy of the original without the qualities of the original, often used in the discussion of simulated realities.

The Matrix *is a SIMULACRUM of reality just like how my ex's new boyfriend is a simulcrum of me.*

spambot *(noun)*
A computer program that automatically sends out spam via e-mail.

A SPAMBOT is not, unfortunately, a robot that dispenses the food product Spam.

Streamy Awards *(proper noun)*
Awards given out by the International Academy of Web Television for excellence in web television, sometimes referred to as "The Streamys."

Between Two Ferns with Zach Galifianakis *won a STREAMY AWARD, and rightly so. It is hilarious.*

streetspotting *(noun)*
The hobby of searching and viewing Google Maps for interesting or humorous images.

Did you see that STREETSPOTTING image of the guys dressed as Wayne and Garth?

synesthesia *(noun)*
A neurological phenomenon where a person's sense are mixed so that a person might smell a sound or see colors in letters.

Jimi Hendrix, someone with SYNESTHESIA, sees color in sound, which explains why his music is so awesome.

technological singularity *(noun)*
When society fundamentally changes as a result of an incredible advancement in technology.

> *The TECHNOLOGICAL SINGULARITY sounds great. As if there weren't already a shortage of jobs.*

technosexual *(noun)*
A person with an obssessive love of machinery and technology.

> *Sheldon Cooper on* The Big Bang Theory *is the ultimate TECHNOSEXUAL.*

texture mapping *(noun)*
To add surface detail and texture to a 3D model.

> Monsters, Inc. *had incredible TEXTURE MAPPING on the furry character Sulley.*

theory of everything *(noun)*
An all-encompassing, yet currently nonexisting theory in physics that can explain, connect, and predict all physical phenomena. It is the Holy Grail of physics.

> *Dude, we are all like One, you know what I mean? Have you ever heard of the THEORY OF EVERYTHING? The trees, the birds, Doritos—everything is connected.*

troll *(noun)*
An annoying person on the Internet that is usually trying to be annoying.

> *Don't feed the TROLL. He's just looking for attention.*

Turing test *(noun)*
A test developed by Alan Turing to determine whether a machine can be said to have intelligence. The test involves a human talking to an anonymous source that is, in fact, a computer. If the human reasonably believes he is speaking with a human and not a computer, then the computer has demonstrated intelligence. At present, this test cannot be met, and some speculate that it can never be satisfied.

> *I use the TURING TEST to determine if I am being instant messaged by a spambot.*

twatted *(verb)*
Past tense for posting something on Twitter.

Sarah Palin famously TWATTED the made-up word "refudiate" and received a lot of backlash. But what else would you expect from a twit like her?

tweet up *(noun)*
To meet up with an acquaintance from Twitter in real life.

Hey Jenny, if you're not an "identity tourist," why don't we TWEET UP this weekend?

twitterati *(noun)*
Twitter power users who attract thousands of followers.

The most popular TWITTERATIs are Ashton Kutcher and Barack Obama.

Vaguebook *(noun)*
To leave a vague update on Facebook with the hope of getting attention.

Examples of attention-grabbing VAGUEBOOK updates, "Hungry. Don't know what to eat . . ." "What's the easiest way to kill yourself?" and "Anyone know the penalty in this state for streaking?"

vaporware *(noun)*
A product that is not released until long after its announced release date or is announced and then never released. A famous vaporware is the game *Duke Nukem Forever*, which has been in development for over twelve years.

Bush's big "Mission Accomplished" announcement was a classic case of VAPORWARE in action.

Voynich manuscript *(noun)*
An untranslated ciphered codex from around the fifteenth century with illustrations describing natural phenomena such as plants, biology, and pharmacology. Known as "the world's most mysterious manuscript."

Tom Hanks should totally play the guy who translates the VOYNICH MANUSCRIPT. "Mama always said this codex was like a box of chocolates—you never know what you're gonna get."

warez *(noun)*
Software or any product that is distributed online in violation of copyright or patent law.

I have never searched for WAREZ in my entire life. I swear.

zettabyte *(noun)*
A unit of digital information that is 1 sextillion bytes, or 10^{21}.

A ZETTABYTE is equivalent to the number of grains of sand on the Earth or the number of known stars.

Chapter 6

GEEKS WATCH ESPN: SPORTS

While sports is not thought of as a particularly geeky activity, especially for those still in high school, geeks are increasingly being drawn to sports; not necessarily playing sports, but in viewing sports and in compiling and analyzing various aspects of sports and sporting data. For example, a sports fan can become a geek by intensely focusing on statistics, history, memorabilia, and game strategies, particularly with respect to fantasy sports leagues. If you want to see some real sports geeks in action, go to a casino sports book in Las Vegas, any time night or day, and observe the denizens.

ABA *(proper noun)*
Short for American Basketball Association. A rival league to the NBA that existed from 1967 to 1976. It eventually merged with the NBA. Known for being more flashy, it featured famous players such as Julius Erving and Moses Malone and used a three-point line and a red, white, and blue ball.
The ABA was far more successful than the XFL.

and one *(phrase)*
A term used when a basketball player scores and also is fouled, allowing the player to shoot a foul shot for an extra point.
AND ONE! Dwayne Wade is fouled while making a shot, giving his team a chance to tie the game with one second left.

ankle breaker *(noun)*
A crossover dribble move in basketball that causes the defender to "break his ankles" trying to keep up.
Allen Iverson was the king of the ANKLE BREAKER, and he even crossed over Michael Jordan.

around the horn *(phrase)*
A baseball term for throwing the ball from first base to second to the shortstop to third base and then the pitcher after an out has been recorded, just for practice.
Going AROUND THE HORN in Little League can often be quite challenging.

audible *(noun)*
A football term for when the play is changed at the line of scrimmage as the quarterback yells out a new play.
Willie Beamen annoys Al Pacino with his AUDIBLES in the movie Any Given Sunday.

autopick *(noun)*
In fantasy sports, when a player can't make a selection in a draft and his or her pick is made automatically. A player should rank draft picks so that favorites are picked.
If you choose AUTOPICK without ranking your players first, you will end up with a team full of Mark Madsens.

GEEK QUIZ

Sports fans have been around for centuries. What is the name of the sports ball that is referred to by William Shakespeare in his play *Henry V*?

a. Badminton

b. Tennis

c. Golf

d. Cricket

Answer: b

Bambino (*proper noun*)
Nickname for Babe Ruth, the greatest baseball player to ever live. Changed baseball into a power game of home runs without using the juice.

Want some pizzerino, Mr. BAMBINO?

BCS (*proper noun*)
Short for Bowl Championship Series, the NCAA football system for determining team ranking and who plays whom in the bowl games. The BCS uses polls as well as computer programs to determine the rankings and matchups.

The BCS has come under a lot of scrutiny, and even President Obama has stated opposition to it.

beanball (*noun*)
A baseball pitch aimed at the batter's body or head.

After being hit with a BEANBALL, a batter will often charge the pitcher's mound.

GEEK FACT

Geek Confession
I once threw nine beanballs in a season as a Little League pitcher. Luckily, eight of the players survived.
—GB

bench clearer *(noun)*

A brawl in sports where the players on the bench join in the fight on the court, playing field, or ice. As seen in the famous Pacers versus Pistons brawl.

The top five BENCH CLEARERS are Pacers vs. Pistons, Braves vs. Padres, Ohio State vs. Minnesota, University of Miami vs. Florida International University, and every time a soccer match is played in England.

Big Show *(proper noun)*

An affectionate term for Major League Baseball.

My friend almost made it to the BIG SHOW. Now, he works at Wal-Mart.

GEEK QUOTE

"I was in the show for twenty-one days once. Best twenty-one days of my life."

—KEVIN COSTNER AS "CRASH" DAVIS IN THE MOVIE *BULL DURHAM*

birdcage *(noun)*

A football term for the helmet of a lineman, which contains extra bars.

The player grabbed the BIRDCAGE and was called for a facemask penalty.

blindside *(noun)*

The term in football for the side opposite to where the quarterback is facing. Also a Sandra Bullock "Oscar bait" film.

Rejected title before choosing The BLINDSIDE *was "Dude, Where's Your Home?"*

blue chip *(noun)*

A top prospect high school player being recruited by college teams.

Shaquille O'Neal was a big-time BLUE CHIP recruit.

GEEK FACT

Other kinds of "chips":
Red chips: Large Chinese public companies
Corn chips: A kind of fatty snack
Shoulder chips: A kind of psychological condition in which one is desperate to prove him or herself

Boom! *(noun)*
A word used by John Madden when there was a huge hit in a football game.
The word BOOM might have been around before John Madden. Then again, he's pretty damned old.

Boom! Goes the dynamite *(phrase)*
Sports catch phrase of Brian Collins, a college sportscaster who made the worst sportscast ever, which became an Internet sensation.
Ray Allen shoots the three and BOOM! GOES THE DYANAMITE!

bootleg *(noun)*
When a quarterback fakes a handoff and runs the other way to throw a pass to a receiver.
A BOOTLEG is also used to denote the kind of DVD movies 90 percent of the players buy.

BPA *(noun)*
Short for best player available. During the NBA draft, always take the best player available, and don't draft for need. The Trailblazers drafted Sam Bowie because they needed a big man and passed on Michael Jordan. Do I have to say it? Epic fail.
Blazers should have chosen the BPA, because no one is singing, "Like Sam. I could be like Sam. I want to be I want to be like Sam."

Brazilian jiu-jitsu *(noun)*
A martial art used successfully in MMA fighting that focuses on ground fighting and certain holds so that a smaller opponent can defeat a larger one.
Royce Gracie, one of the originators of the UFC, is a practiced BRAZILLIAN JIU-JITSU expert and a UFC Hall-of-Famer.

Bronx cheer *(noun)*
A baseball term for when the crowd boos a team or player.
Every time my wife and I have sex, she lets out a cheer . . . a BRONX CHEER.

bush league *(noun)*
A player who is inferior and belongs in the minor leagues.
"This BUSH LEAGUE psyche-out stuff. Laughable, man – ha ha!"
– Jesus, in The Big Lebowski

bust *(noun)*
A drafted player who fails to reach his potential, even though drafted very high.
JaMarcus Russell was drafted number one by the Raiders and was paid a lot of money, but he never lived up to expectations and has been labeled a BUST.

Candyslam *(proper noun)*
The name of one of Darryl Dawkins's dunks. Other names include In Your Face Disgrace, Earthquaker Shaker, Dunk You Very Much, Yo Mama, Turbo Sexophonic Delight, and the Rim Wrecker.
Before that dude tries the CANDYSLAM, he might want to master the candy lay-up.

chaingang *(noun)*
Assistants to football officials that mark off the yards necessary for a first down.
> *The CHAINGANG runs onto the field and after measuring with their chain . . . it's a first down by a hair!*

charity stripe *(noun)*
Another word for the foul line in basketball.
> *When Shaquille O'Neal lines up to shoot a foul shot at the CHARITY STRIPE, it always turns out to be like giving charity—to the opposing team!*

chess boxing *(noun)*
A sport where players box one round and then play chess the next round.
> *CHESS BOXING will match our brains and brawn, and will determine who is truly the master of the universe.*

GEEK QUIZ

If you are tall, then you have an advantage in basketball, which is why the NBA goes after the tallest players. But sometimes the smaller players can make it as well. Who is the shortest NBA player of all time at 5'3"?

a. Muggsy Bogues

b. Earl Boykins

c. Spud Webb

d. Nate "Tiny" Archibald

Answer: a

---

chin music *(noun)*
In baseball, when the pitcher throws the ball near or at the batter's face.
> *When a pitcher becomes frustrated, the batter might expect a little CHIN MUSIC.*

chippy *(adjective)*
Used in basketball and hockey to describe a physical atmosphere on the court or ice.
> *Boy, it sure is CHIPPY out there isn't it? The refs are letting them play.*

church music *(noun)*
A term in basketball for a soft jump shot that hits nothing but net.
> *That jump shot was soft as CHURCH MUSIC. I'm not much of a religious man, but that was just divine.*

Cinderella story *(noun)*
Used in sports to describe an underdog that makes it further than thought possible. Made famous by Bill Murray in a classic line in *Caddyshack*.
> *The 2008 Arizona Cardinals only had a 9-7 record in the regular season but managed to defeat many of the favorite teams and became a CINDERELLA STORY before eventually losing at the last second to the Pittsburgh Steelers.*

clinic *(noun)*
A display of extraordinary sports ability.
> *Tyreke Evens of the Sacramento Kings is putting on a shooting CLINIC!*

cupcake *(noun)*
When a basketball team has a schedule full of easy opponents.
> *Ohio State has a CUPCAKE schedule this year.*

The Curse *(noun)*
The curse of the Billy Goat. When Billy Sianis had to leave a Cubs game because his pet goat was too smelly, he said, "Them Cubs, they aren't gonna win no more." This curse supposedly has prevented the Cubs from getting to the World Series since 1945.
> *The Red Sox also had a CURSE, the curse of the Bambino, but that was broken when they won the 2004 World Series.*

crunch time *(noun)*
A sports term for the end of a game, when the outcome has not yet been determined.
> *Come on, guys. You want to win this thing or not? It's CRUNCH TIME!*

diaper dandy *(noun)*
A young college basketball player who is amazing as a freshman.
> *The NBA is getting younger and younger these days, with more and more DIAPER DANDIES declaring for the draft.*

Dream Team *(proper noun)*
The nickname for the USA basketball team in the 1992 Olympics that won the gold medal. The team included Michael Jordan, Magic Johnson, Larry Bird, and many other Hall-of-Famers.
> *The term DREAM TEAM is also used to denote the amazing team of lawyers who helped get the obviously guilty O. J. Simpson acquitted of brutally murdering his ex-wife and her lover.*

GEEK QUOTE

Bill Murray: It's 'cause I'm white, isn't it?
Michael Jordan: No. Larry's white. So what?
Bill Murray: Larry's not white. Larry's clear.

—FROM THE 1996 MOVIE *SPACE JAM*

drift *(verb)*
While racing in a car, to oversteer so that the car loses traction and slides in a turn.
> *DRIFTING is also known as "dying."*

dropping dimes *(verb)*
A basketball term for when a player is dishing out a lot of assists. Not to be confused with dropping loads.
> *Steve Nash was DROPPING DIMES in that game against the Lakers.*

duck fart *(noun)*
A soft hit in baseball that goes over the infielder's head for a single.
> *He is a great baseball player, king of the DUCK FARTS.*

dying quail *(noun)*
A hit ball in baseball that drops suddenly like a shot bird in front of the fielder.

The outfielder backed up, thinking the ball would reach the fence, but it was a DYING QUAIL and dropped ten feet in front of him.

dynasty *(noun)*
When a sports team dominates a sport for a long period of time. Examples: the L.A. Lakers, the Boston Celtics, the New England Patriots, the San Francisco 49ers, and the New York Yankees.

The Miami Heat is attempting to create a new DYNASTY with the signing of LeBron James, Dwayne Wade, and Chris Bosh.

encroachment *(noun)*
A football foul that occurs when a player crosses the line of scrimmage before the ball is snapped.

The Raiders just keep racking up the penalties, the latest an ENCROACHMENT call leading to a five-yard offsides penalty.

enforcer *(noun)*
A player on a hockey team that is unofficially responsible for fighting or checking another player in response to an aggressive or violent move.

Don't hate the ENFORCER; hate the game.

Fab Five *(proper noun)*
The starting five players on the University of Michigan's basketball team in 1992 and 1993 that reached the title game. Included Chris Webber, Jalen Rose, and Juwan Howard.

Whenever my buddies and I play basketball we use the phrase FAB FIVE to describe any opponents we play. Makes us feel better when we inevitably lose.

facial *(noun)*
In basketball, when a shooter slam dunks the rock right in the defender's face.

We often wonder where basketball announcers found their inspiration for the FACIAL metaphor.

fantasy football *(noun)*
A fantasy league game played by football fans, where the fans draft players onto teams and then play opposing teams. Points are determined mostly by the individual statistical accomplishments of each player during the week.

My only escape from reality is my FANTASY FOOTBALL league.

Final Four *(proper noun)*
In the NCAA Men's Division I Basketball Championship tournament, these are the surviving four teams (the winners of each region) remaining out of the original group, which includes sixty-eight teams beginning in 2011. One of the Final Four will go on to win the championship.

A good performance in the FINAL FOUR can enhance a player's draft prospects.

flood *(noun)*
A football term for sending more players to a certain area to gain a strategic advantage. A flood is a great strategy against a zone defense, forcing the defense to guard multiple players.

There's no FLOOD insurance in a football game.

flop *(verb)*
To fake being fouled (requires good acting).

Vlade Divac was known as being a very talented FLOP artist but also was a great basketball player.

GEEK QUIZ

The XFL was a professional football league created by Vince McMahon to compete with the NFL. It included stars such as Rod "He Hate Me" Smart and made all the following rule changes *except*:

a. No fair catch

b. No overtime

c. No extra point kicks

d. Race to determine kick-off

Answer: b

---

franchise player (noun)
A player on an NFL, NBA, or NHL team may be so designated when the player is the "face" of the team. Typically, the player will have a multiple-year contract.

In the NFL, a FRANCHISE PLAYER may not be able to enter free agency and must be paid a contractually determined salary.

free agent (noun)
A professional athlete who is free from his or her contract and has the ability to sign with any team desired. A restricted free agent's old team can match a new offer from another team and retain the player, while an unrestricted free agent can sign with another team without that restriction.

FREE AGENT LeBron James stunned the basketball world last summer when he opted to "take his talents to South Beach" and play for the Miami Heat in "The Decision."

free running (noun)
Also "freerunning," a form of urban acrobatics where participants run through the city using various parts of the landscape—stairways, benches, walls, awnings, elevator shafts—as obstacles. Although it was inspired by Parkour (see below), free running emphasizes complete freedom of movement and acrobatics. A famous example of free running was in the 2006 James Bond film *Casino Royale,* when Agent 007 chases free runner Sébastien Foucan through a Madagascar construction site.

Watching a skilled FREE RUNNER is like watching Spider-Man on the ground—only without the webs and super powers.

French pastry (noun)
A fancy pass in basketball.

That around-the-back elbow pass by Jason Williams was a real FRENCH PASTRY!

Friendly Confines (noun)
Wrigley Field in Chicago.

Wrigley Field was first called the FRIENDLY CONFINES by Mr. Cub, Ernie Banks.

Game of the Century *(proper noun)*
An NCAA basketball game played by the University of Houston Cougars and the UCLA Bruins in 1968 that was the first NCAA game broadcast on television nationwide during prime time. Houston ended up beating UCLA 71 to 69.

The GAME OF THE CENTURY is said to have started nationwide interest in watching college basketball on television.

Goal of the Century *(proper noun)*
In the 1986 World Cup, a goal by Diego Maradona, considered the greatest of all time, where Diego maneuvered around multiple opponents (including the goalie) before scoring.

Maradona made the GOAL OF THE CENTURY after he scored the "Hand of God" goal. This second goal turned out to be the game-winner for Argentina. And yes, this time he decided to use his foot instead of his hand.

GOAT *(noun)*
Short for greatest of all time, it is used to describe the greatest player of a sport, such as Michael Jordan for basketball. Also the nickname of the legendary streetball player Earl Manigault, who was only 6'1" but supposedly could grab a dollar off the top of a backboard and replace it with change.

Kareem Abdul-Jabbar said the GOAT, Earl Manigault, was the greatest player he has ever played with or against.

GEEK QUIZ

What is the name of the golfer that first used the word "caddy" while playing golf?

a. Harry Vardon

b. Mary Queen of Scots

c. King James II

d. Sir Walter Cronkite

Answer: b

---

golden sombrero *(noun)*

When a player has four strikeouts in one baseball game. Three strikeouts are considered a hat trick. Four strikeouts is a giant hat, or a sombrero.

On some very tough teams, the coach will instruct the players to give a golden shower to a player wearing a GOLDEN SOMBRERO.

goose egg *(noun)*

When a sports team has a zero on the scoreboard during a game.

At the end of the game we had GOOSE EGG on the scoreboard.

grand slam *(noun)*

In baseball, a homerun with the bases loaded. When a player wins all of the major tournaments in a single year in tennis (U.S. Open, Wimbledon, French Open, and Australian Open) or in golf (The Masters, U.S. Open, British Open, PGA Championship).

The GRAND SLAM is also a dish at Denny's that is edible from about 3 a.m. to 4 a.m..

hack-a-Shaq *(noun)*

A strategy used in NBA basketball to continually foul Shaquille O'Neal, a notoriously bad free-throw shooter. Used mostly at the end of a game, when each possession is more valuable.

The HACK-A-SHAQ technique might be effective, but it's boring as hell to watch.

Hand of God *(proper noun)*

In the 1986 World Cup, a goal by Diego Maradona of Argentina against England using his hand, which was not called a handball by the referees.

A second HAND OF GOD incident occurred in a game between France and the Republic of Ireland during the 2010 FIFA World Cup playoff, which has been called the "Hand of Frog."

hang ten *(verb)*

To surf at the front of the board with your toes sticking off the edge.

As stated in Apocalypse Now, *a HANG TEN can best be done on an old-fashioned longboard.*

GEEK QUIZ

Nicknames in sports can define how a player plays or is perceived. You haven't made it in sports until you have a nickname. Which is *not* a nickname that has been used in sports?

a. Andrei Kirilenko "AK-47"

b. Rafer Alston: "Skip 2 My Lou"

c. "The Gaye One" Gaye Stewart

d. Karl "The Postman" Malone

Answer: d

Homerun Derby *(proper noun)*
An event that takes place during Major League Baseball's All-Star Weekend, where players compete to see who can hit the most home runs.
With 41 homers in 2005, Bobby Abreu is the all-time king of the HOMERUN DERBY.

hot dog *(noun)*
A show-off ball hog in a basketball game. Also, a kind of freestyle snow skiing noted for its acrobatics.
Famous HOT DOGs are Michael Jordan, Kobe Bryant, LeBron James—basically anyone really good.

hurry-up offense *(noun)*
A football offensive strategy that uses as little time off the clock as possible on each down; also known as the no-huddle offense. It was used successfully by Jim Kelly of the Buffalo Bills, who reached the Super Bowl four times in a row and then decided it would be more fun to lose.
Typical features of the HURRY-UP OFFENSE include audibles and running out of bounds to stop the clock.

in the zone *(phrase)*
To lose oneself in a mental state of perfect energy, focus, involvement, and success. In other words, to be in a flow, succeeding in achieving a perfect balance between ability and challenge, as described by Mihály Csíkszentmihályi in his book *Flow*.
When Ray Allen hit seven three-pointers in a row during the 2010 finals, he was IN THE ZONE.

jay *(verb)*

In basketball, to hit a jump shot, preferably over a shot blocker.

> *In the 2001 Western conference finals, Robert Horry JAYED a 3 to drive a dagger into the hearts of the Sacramento Kings.*

Jesus Shuttlesworth *(proper noun)*

A nickname for Ray Allen, NBA player for the Boston Celtics, derived from his blue chip basketball player character in the Spike Lee movie *He Got Game.*

> *JESUS SHUTTLESWORTH with the trey!*

Lew Alcindor Rule *(proper noun)*

A rule named after Kareem Abdul-Jabbar, whose birthname was Ferdinand Lewis "Lew" Alcindor Jr. The rule banned dunking in the NCAA from 1967 to 1976, probably because of his dominating dunkage.

> *I have followed the no-dunk LEW ALCINDOR RULE my entire life.*

lollipop *(noun)*

A baseball term for a short pitch or weak throw.

> *Get that little six-year-old girl outta there! She's been throwin' LOLLIPOPS all day!*

Malice at the Palace *(proper noun)*

The brawl between the Pistons and the Pacers, where a fan threw a cup of soda that hit Ron Artest and started a fan versus player fight.

> *The first fan to get punched by Ron Artest at the MALICE AT THE PALACE went from jovial to deathly afraid when Ron confronted him in the stands and he realized Ron thought he was the guy that threw the soda.*

mid-level exception *(noun)*

The once-a-year ability of NBA teams to sign a player to the average salary even if they are over the salary cap.

> *Ron Artest signed to the Los Angeles Lakers in 2009 for their MID-LEVEL EXCEPTION and helped them win a championship the next year.*

GEEK QUIZ

Some sports teams have names that inspire more fear than others. The Utah Jazz is not necessarily an intimidating sounding team name. What is *not* the name of a real sports team?

a. Webster University Gorloks

b. Centralia Orphans

c. Butte Pirates

d. Camarillo Shoehorns

Midsummer Classic *(proper noun)*
The term for the Major League Baseball All-Star Game, where players are selected by the fans to compete against each other. The team that wins, either the National League or the American League, has home field advantage in the World Series.

A continuing controversy of the MIDSUMMER CLASSIC is that every team must be represented, causing some to believe there are players who are not worthy of the honor.

no-drop list *(noun)*
In fantasy sports, players on this list cannot be dropped. This prevents collusion, where a player drops good atheletes so they can be picked up by another player.

I want to be put on the NO-DROP LIST at my job.

noseriding *(verb)*
To "hang ten." This is surfing at the front of the board with all ten toes sticking off the edge.

My girlfriend was NOSERIDING the board before she wiped out.

octagon *(noun)*
The cage used by fighters in the UFC.

I'm not sure why they named it the OCTAGON, though. Might have something to do with eight sides or something.
Nah. They probably named it after the Chuck Norris movie.

ollie *(noun)*
Skateboarding trick invented by Allan "Ollie" Gelfland in 1978 where, the skater, without using his or her hands, jumps in the air with the board coming completely off the ground.

It takes a lot of practice to get an OLLIE down, but once you do, all the other tricks come much easier.

painting the black *(phrase)*
A baseball pitch on the edge of the plate, which is made of black rubber.

Casey swung and missed because the pitcher was PAINTING THE BLACK.

parkour *(noun)*
People running and jumping over obstacles in a fluid manner, such as an urban environment. See also *free running*.

PARKOUR is useful for anyone running from the cops.

Paul the Octopus *(proper noun)*
A soothsaying German octopus that became a 2010 World Cup phenomenon due to his correct predictions.

PAUL THE OCTOPUS has magical powers. I must eat him to gain his powers.

Pelé *(proper noun)*
The nickname of Brazilian Edison Arantes do Nascimento, the world's greatest soccer player ever. Pelé was an amazing scorer and won three World Cups. He scored 6 goals as a seventeen-year-old in the World Cup.

PELÉ may have been the greatest player of all time, but Beckham looks better in his underwear.

pentathlon *(noun)*
An Olympic event that includes fencing, shooting, swimming, horse riding, and running.

The PENTATHLON of the geek-Olympics would feature GoldenEye 007, World of Warcraft, Magic: The Gathering, *programming, and comic book trivia.*

GEEK FACT

Pelé costarred in the 1981 film *Escape to Victory* (known simply as *Victory* in North America), directed by famed director John Huston. The story concerns Allied prisoners in a World War II German internment camp. The film starred Sylvester Stallone, Michael Caine, and Max von Sydow, but many of the other prisoners were played by football (that's soccer to you Yanks) superstars. During a climactic scene, Pelé scores a goal against the German team by leaping in the air, flipping upside down, and kicking a goal, without using special effects. He really did it.

Phi Slama Jama *(proper noun)*
The nickname for University of Houston Cougars basketball team from 1982 to 1984. They played more of a streetball style and always made it to the Final Four. Included Clyde Drexler and Hakeem Olajuwon.
When Clyde the Glide and Hakeem the Dream played on the Houston Rockets, it was a PHI SLAMA JAMA reunion.

GEEK FACT

Street-Style Versus Court-Style Basketball
Court Style:
  Foul: Anything that unfairly prohibits the shooter from making a basket (such as hitting his arm or hands, jumping in his way when he has momentum, and so forth)
Street Style:
  Foul: Anything that unfairly prohibits the shooter from making a basket involving an illegal firearm
Court Style:
  Stealing: Taking the ball from the opponent
Street Style:
  Stealing: What the players do when they are NOT playing basketball
Court Style:
  Slam dunk: Slamming the ball down through the hoop
Street Style:
  Slam dunk: What players say when they pass the GED

The Play *(proper noun)*
A famous college football play where the Cal Bears (University of California, Berkeley Golden Bears) won against Stanford in the 1982 big game on a final kickoff return that was unbelievable in the number of laterals and the fact that Cal also had to get around Stanford's band that was on the field celebrating prematurely.

Many people wrongly believe that, during THE PLAY, one of the Cal Bears' returners was actually down at the 17 before he got off the lateral that won the game.

play-action pass *(noun)*
A fake handoff by a quarterback who then proceeds to drop back to pass the ball.

A PLAY-ACTION PASS is the exact opposite of a draw play, which is to fake a pass and then hand the ball off to a running back.

play by the book *(phrase)*
A term in sports for when a player or team needs to get back to basics and not do anything fancy or risky.

Tim Duncan is a great player and also known for being one to PLAY BY THE BOOK.

The Professor *(proper noun)*
Nickname of Grayson Boucher, a streetball player and star of the AND1 Mixtape Tour.

THE PROFESSOR is also famous for being the only white player on the AND1 team.

pylons *(noun)*
1. In football, small orange foam markers at the four corners of the end zone. 2. In *Starcraft*, pylons are protoss structures used to warp in buildings.

In football, a pass is not completed if caught outside the PYLONS.

riding the pine *(phrase)*
A sports term for sitting on the bench and not playing.

Mark Madsen is known for RIDING THE PINE.

right down Broadway *(phrase)*
A baseball pitch that is thrown directly in the middle of the strike zone.
Swing batta batta swing! Send one RIGHT DOWN BROADWAY!

GEEK QUIZ

Kobe Bryant scored 81 points in one game recently, but surprisingly, that was only the second most points that have been scored in one game. What NBA player holds the record for the most points in a game, with 100 points, and also has bragged to have slept with 20,000 women?

a. Bill Russell

b. Jerry West

c. Wilt Chamberlain

d. Mark Madsen

Answer: c

---

rip *(verb)*
A steal in basketball.
John Stockton is known for having the most RIPS of all time with 3,265.

rock *(noun)*
A basketball.
Pass the ROCK!

role player *(noun)*
A player on a basketball team who is not a star but plays a minor but important role in winning. Role players are needed for a team to be a championship contender.
Examples of NBA ROLE PLAYERS include Steve Kerr, Glen "Big Baby" Davis, and Allen Iverson late in his career, although he still thinks of himself as the number one star.

salary cap *(noun)*

The upper limit that a professional sports team can pay all of their players in the aggregate without incurring a luxury tax. Without a salary cap, a rich team might be able to get all of the league's highest-paid players on a single team.

In 2010, the Miami Heat freed up enough SALARY CAP room to sign three maximum-contract players in Dwayne Wade, Chris Bosh, and LeBron James.

scrimmage *(noun)*

A practice game in sports.

The first Iraq War was a SCRIMMAGE. The second Iraq war was the real showdown.

SI curse *(noun)*

The myth that when an athlete appears on the cover of *Sports Illustrated*, he or she will have bad luck afterward. Those who have unfortunately been struck with the curse include Pete Rose, Brett Favre, and Olympic star Lindsey Vonn.

One way to evade the SI CURSE is to continue not playing a professional sport.

sky flying *(noun)*

An activity involving a skydiver or base jumper who wears a wing suit, which is designed to give the wearer's body more surface area through the design of the suit, much like a flying squirrel, so that he or she can glide through the air.

Can I get a SKY FLYING ticket for my trip to New York this weekend?

slurve *(noun)*

A baseball pitch that is a slow-breaking curve ball.

If you're throwing me the remote control, make sure you don't SLURVE it.

spread *(noun)*

In sports betting, a spread is the predicted difference in the final scores of two teams. Gamblers bet whether the actual difference in the final scores is over or under the spread.

The SPREAD is adjusted so that there is an equal amount of people betting on each side of the spread.

stiff *(noun)*
A tall basketball player who may be tall but has no real skills.
Shawn Bradley is the ultimate STIFF. He is featured in many posters being dunked on.

spear, spearing *(verb)*
In football, to hit another player using the top of your helmet.
Houston Oilers running back Earl Campbell was an expert in SPEARING.

stunt pogo *(noun)*
An extreme sport done while on a pogo stick, with tricks such as backflips or 360s. You can compete at stunt pogo at Pogopalooza.
Me and the boys like to STUNT POGO just to be hardcore.

three-peat *(noun)*
A sports term, trademarked by former Lakers coach Pat Riley, that means a team has won three championships in a row.
Careful. The term THREE-PEAT has actually been copyrighted by Pat Riley. You now owe him a quarter just for thinking it.

tools of ignorance *(noun)*
A baseball catcher's paraphenalia.
If catchers wear the TOOLS OF IGNORANCE, then why are they the ones who tell the pitcher what to throw and where to throw it?

triangle offense *(noun)*
An offensive scheme used famously by Phil Jackson with the Chicago Bulls and the Los Angeles Lakers. It creates a triangle using the center, the power forward, and a guard. The other guard is at the top of the key and the small forward is at the weak-side high post.
Other teams have tried to implement the TRIANGLE OFFENSE, but without much success. The fact that they don't have Michael Jordan or Kobe Bryant might have something to do with it.

tube ride *(noun)*
A move in surfing, where when the wave is breaking, there is an inner area like a tube in which the surfer can ride.
Surfing may be too difficult to TUBE RIDE at first, so try doing it while body surfing.

turkey *(noun)*
A bowling term used to denote a player getting three strikes in a row. The term was coined in the nineteenth century when, during the holiday season, whoever threw three strikes in a row would win a free turkey.

You might be down a ton of points to your opponent, but there is always a chance at getting a TURKEY.

vuvuzela *(noun)*
A horn that emits a deep monotone sound, used heavily in the 2010 World Cup games.

The VUVUZELA is not appreciated by anyone who isn't South African and isn't blowing into a VUVUZELA.

weak sauce *(noun)*
A derogatory term for a person or a sports player who performs at a substandard level or, in the vernacular, sucks.

WEAK SAUCE is every player on the Knicks.

wet *(adjective)*
Describes a jumpshot in basketball that is a swish (nothing but net).

Damn, I never seen you so WET!

white-knuckler *(noun)*
A close sports game that comes down to the wire.

Every soccer match seems to be a WHITE KNUCKLER.

GEEK FACT

Best White-Knuckler of All Time: "Miracle on Ice"
In the 1980 Olympics, the United States defeated the heavily favored Soviet Union in one of the most famous ice hockey matches in history. What most people don't remember is that this wasn't the gold medal game. The United States had to beat Finland in the following game to earn the gold medal.

Who dat? *(phrase)*
A chant by New Orleans Saints fans that may have originated as a sports chant in the 1960s by fans of the Southern University Jaguars.

WHO DAT? WHO DAT? WHO DAT say dey gonna beat dem Saints?

wild card *(noun)*
In football, the two playoff spots given to teams with the best record that didn't win their divisions.
  The New York Giants were a WILD CARD team that won the Super Bowl in 2008.

wildcat formation *(noun)*
An offensive formation in football where the ball is snapped to a player such as a running back rather than to the quarterback.
  Atlanta Falcons receiver Tim Dwight takes the direct snap in the 1998 NFC championships and runs for twenty yards in a perfect execution of the WILDCAT FORMATION.

worm burner *(noun)*
A ground ball in baseball that moves very fast.
  I couldn't get to the ball; it was a real WORM BURNER.

X Games *(proper noun)*
A competition for extreme sports held by ESPN since 1995 that features skateboarding, motocross, rally car racing, and snowboarding in the winter games.
  Tony Hawk has won 9 X GAMES gold medals.

Chapter 7

GEEKED UP ON D&D: GAMING

Now we get to real hardcore geek territory: gaming. Nothing is more common than a teenage geek who spends all his or her free time playing video games, role-playing games like *Dungeons & Dragons,* or online games such as *World of Warcraft.* Contrary to popular belief, games have many positive aspects, such as helping the player develop problem-solving and hand-eye coordination skills, providing the player with a sense of participation and achievement, encouraging the player to think creatively, and helping the player avoid spending time with his or her family. Many geeks have warm memories of gathering together with their friends to play video games such as *Mario Kart,* or *Medal of Honor* if they needed to expunge some "aggression." But the point is, it's a geek activity that is social in nature and involves interacting with other people, even if only virtually, so grab your controller or polyhedral dice, and let the pwnage begin!

1-up *(noun)*

Gaining an extra life in a video game.

The 1-UP first appeared in the 1970s in pinball games.

8-bit music *(noun)*

A genre in electronic music that mimics songs in 8-bit video game systems such as the original Nintendo.

The best 8-BIT MUSIC hands-down was the theme song from Legend of Zelda.

AD&D *(proper noun)*

Short for Advanced Dungeons & Dragons. A more advanced and structured version of the Dungeons & Dragons rules, first released in 1977.

In 1977, AD&D separated the boys from the man-boys.

adult fans of LEGO *(noun)*

Adults who enjoy collecting, discussing, and building with LEGO building blocks.

Forget ADULT FANS OF LEGO. Where can I sign up for adult fans of Eggos?

advertise *(verb)*

In games—especially Texas Hold'em—to "advertise" is to make an early move intended to falsely present yourself as a weak player.

ADVERTISING only works when the other players are skillful enough to notice what you are doing.

aggro *(noun)*

Aggression; to be the center of the enemy's attacks in an RPG.

AGGRO, also referred to as "hate," can be used in strategy such as when one player acts as a decoy, drawing most of the enemy attacks, while the other makes moves to attack in a more covert way.

aimbot *(noun)*

A form of cheating in a computer game where a player hacks the game so that every shot he or she fires is a hit. Aimbots are used often in first-person shooters. And some games, such as *GoldenEye 007,* have an aimbot option to help novice players.

Using an AIMBOT can and should result in an instant ban.

alignment *(noun)*

In Dungeons & Dragons, a character's alignment describes where they stand morally and ethically. Alignments range from lawful good to neutral to chaotic evil.

The coolest people's ALIGNMENT was obviously always chaotic neutral. They smoked, dressed in all black, and listened to Dragonforce.

alpha strike *(noun)*

In an RPG, to attack with everything for the win.

Yeah, I think I'm gonna just win now with an ALPHA STRIKE and spare you a drawn-out death.

Ameritrash *(noun)*

The term for boardgames in America that are known for having too many pieces and that involve a lot of direct conflict.

If you call Sorry *an AMERITRASH game, then we're going to have a problem that will make you sorry, for real.*

anticomputer gaming tactic *(noun)*

A type of play used by humans to beat formidable computer opponents at various games, especially boardgames.

An ANTICOMPUTER GAMING TACTIC in Starcraft *is for a terran to build a wall of supply depots because the computer will not attack the depots and will just wait outside, ready to be killed.*

ARG *(noun)*

Short for alternative-reality game. A game played in the real world in real time that uses cell phones, e-mail, and the Internet. It is often used as a promotional medium for films and other media.

When you are in an ARG, remember its motto: "This is not a game."

attributes *(noun)*

In AD&D, the set of statistics that make up a character. It includes strength, dexterity, constitution, intelligence, wisdom, and charisma. If you have a lot of charisma, you can be ugly but still persuade people to do what you want.

ATTRIBUTES of Bill Gates include a low strength score but a wisdom score that is off the charts.

Atari *(proper noun)*
Company that produced arcade games such as Pong in 1972 and the Atari 2600 game console in 1977. When they released a ported version of Pac-Man, it sucked so bad it contributed to a video game industry crash in 1983. Interestingly, Atari secretly created a pinball and arcade competitor company called Kee Games, founded by friends of theirs, in response to distributors wanting exclusive deals.
Every morning before school, I used to play ATARI.

BADD *(proper noun)*
Short for Bothered About Dungeons & Dragons; a group started by Patricia Pulling after her son committed suicide. According to Pulling, her son killed himself because he thought he had a curse placed on him related to the game.
I've never heard of BADD, but I've heard of Color Me Badd, *unfortunately.*

beat 'em up *(noun)*
A video game genre where the player walks around and beats others up. That is the whole game. The player's character usually wears a bandana and a denim jacket. Examples: *Double Dragon, Final Fight,* and *Golden Axe.*
BEAT 'EM UP is like a video game version of the movie The Warriors.

beta tester *(noun)*
A player who receives a game before it has been released to test it out for bugs, try the gameplay, and give feedback to the developer.
Ronny lucked out by getting to be a Blizzard BETA TESTER.

BFG 9000 *(proper noun)*
A devastating weapon in the video game *Doom* that obliterates an enemy in one shot.
Being as this is a BFG 9000, the most powerful gun in Doom, *you've got to ask yourself one question: "Do I feel lucky?" Well, do ya, punk?*

bloatware *(noun)*
Extra features installed by software that are unnecessary.
BLOATWARE can be seen in Adobe Reader, which is 26 MB, while other versions that do the same thing are only around 7MB.

bloom effect *(noun)*
Used in computer games to give the appearance of a real camera by adding a glow or light effect.
A BLOOM EFFECT surrounds George Lucas wherever he goes.

body pull *(noun)*
A technique where an RPG player lures an enemy away from a group for a one-on-one battle.
My friend BODY PULLED this guy away from his girl so I could talk to her.

boffer wars *(noun)*
Simulated battles in LARPS that use padded-foam weapons and involve players dressing in a style that matches the LARP, such as medieval garb.
In a BOFFER WAR, there is no prize for being the runner-up.

boss *(noun)*
A major enemy that appears at the end of a video game level that you have to defeat by figuring out his patterns and specific weaknesses. The first boss ever appeared in the 1980 arcade game Phoenix, an outer space shooter.
I could never defeat the BOSS Mike Tyson in Mike Tyson's Punch Out.

brilliancy *(noun)*
A chess game that involves an unusual amount of creativity.
Every chess game I play is a BRILLIANCY.

buff *(verb)*
To increase an element in a game, such as increasing a statistic or feature.
The Mark of the Wild in World of Warcraft *is a BUFF that increases a target's strength, agility, armor, stamina, spirit, intellect, and resistance.*

bunnying *(noun)*
The act of controlling another player in an MMORPG and not playing properly or in a serious manner.
Jim, I am BUNNYING your Warcraft *player and making him randomly strike friendly players. I hope you don't mind.*

button mashing; mashing *(noun)*
When a video game player doesn't know which buttons to press in a fighting game and just presses random buttons.

> *BUTTON MASHING works with Eddy Gordo in* Tekken *very well, although I always won because of skill and not just MASHING.*

Caissa *(proper noun)*
The goddess of chess.

> *CAISSA was first denoted the goddess of chess in a 1763 poem by Sir William Jones.*

campaign *(noun)*
An adventure in an RPG that follows a particular plot line or occurs in a certain world or land.

> *My real-life CAMPAIGN involves a heroic quest to cut calories.*

camper *(noun)*
A derogatory word for a video game player in a first-person shooter who sits in a secret place waiting for people to walk past so that he or she can shoot them. Campers are easy to kill because they are clueless when you sneak up behind them.

> *CAMPERS are annoying in games, but they are actually use a good strategy that is more likely to keep them alive than running around with guns blazing.*

Candy Land *(proper noun)*
A child's game where the players must find the lost king of Candy Land. No strategy or decision making is involved in the game, as the moves are determined by drawn cards.

> *CANDY LAND is good for teaching kids how to play games—and entertaining themselves because daddy is working right now.*

capped *(verb)*
When an RPG character has reached the maximum allowable experience points.

> *Lothar of the Hill People CAPPED his relationship with his wife by both walking very, very far, and very, very fast.*

card counting *(noun)*
A strategy used by card players to keep track of the high and low cards in blackjack. It is done by assigning points to each card to keep a running count to predict what cards will be dealt next.
Rain Man used CARD COUNTING to beat the odds in Las Vegas.

Cavity Sam *(proper noun)*
The red-nosed character being operated on in the game Operation.
CAVITY SAM should file for malpractice.

character class *(noun)*
The identity of a character in an RPG that determines abilities and skills, such as fighter, thief, cleric, druid, bard, and paladin. The character class is chosen at the beginning of the RPG by the player and affects how the game is played from that point forward.
I have a friend that talks incessantly about CHARACTER CLASS. He is such an elitist.

character sheet *(noun)*
A recording of an RPG character's statistics and any other items, background, or details that are necessary to play as the character.
Your CHARACTER SHEET is a lot like your rap sheet.

cheapo *(noun)*
A cheap trick in chess, also known as a swindle.
You are either incredibly smart or incredibly stupid. That move was completely CHEAPO.

GEEK QUIZ

After the success of pen and paper RPGs, it was only natural for them to end up on video game systems. What is the name of the first console-based role-playing game?

a. Dragonstomper

b. Dungeons & Dragons

c. Gnome Master

d. Zork

Answer: a

---

cheat code *(noun)*

Certain buttons or keystrokes that the player presses at the beginning of a video game that allows the player to receive special abilities or jump ahead.

A real life CHEAT CODE would be being born into the Hilton family.

chess variant *(noun)*

A type of game in chess using different rules, adding or subtracting pieces, or using a different-sized board.

We need a CHESS VARIANT that doesn't use the queen. Why? Because she thinks it's all about her.

chew toy *(noun)*

A tough RPG character whose purpose is to absorb most of the damage in a battle, thus diverting attention away from other members of the party.

In Return of the Jedi, *during the battle of Endor, Rebel fleet Star Cruisers were CHEW TOYs for the Death Star while the small Rebel fighters maneuvered so that they could enter the Death Star.*

chromatic abberation *(noun)*

Camera blur effect in video games or CGI to make an image look more realistic.

CHROMATIC ABBERATION is a powerful tool and not to be abused, young grasshopper.

Chrono Trigger *(proper noun)*

An RPG game for the Super NES. It contained unusual and revolutionary aspects such as multiple endings and side quests, although you still fought wandering monsters, which is pretty usual.

Many label CHRONO TRIGGER as one of the best games ever.

chump block *(noun)*

An RPG character that chooses to absorb most of the damage in a battle to help the party but does not have the hit points to survive.

My character was used as a CHUMP BLOCK and died after being hit by a magic missile.

Civilization *(proper noun)*

A 1991 computer game developed by Sid Meier that was a turn-based simulation where the player must develop an empire from ancient history to the future.

CIVILIZATION is one of the most popular game series of all time.

clickie *(noun)*

An item or spell that requires double-clicking to be activated.

So many CLICKIES, so little time!

cloning *(verb)*

To give the same command to many different targets, such as in a strategy game like *Starcraft*.

I keep CLONING all my marines and tanks to attack the Zerg expansion base.

combo *(noun)*

A set of moves in a video game that leads to a superior move.

I was the master of the super COMBO in Street Fighter Alpha.

console wars *(noun)*

A battle between different video game consoles, where both products are released during the same time period and compete in the market, such as the battle between the Sega Genesis and the Super Nintendo,

I sided with Sega in the CONSOLE WARS, but I guess I chose the losing side.

cosplay *(noun)*

Short for costumed roleplay, it is where people dress like characters from movies, video games, or anime.

COSPLAY is better than anime because there are real girls involved.

Covenant *(proper noun)*

The alien alliance in the *Halo* game series. The Covenant is at war with humanity over the Halos, gigantic space structures in the shape of a halo. The Covenant ends up, unknowingly, releasing the Flood, a dangerous parasitic alien.

In Halo 2, *the player can take on the role of one of the COVENANT, making the game more interesting.*

cover system *(noun)*
How a character in a video game dodges and avoids being hit.
> Gears of War *uses a unique COVER SYSTEM that involves ducking and rolling, as well as using incapacitated enemies as body shields.*

crap rare *(noun)*
A game card in Magic: The Gathering that is rare and worth a lot of money but is useless or not at all helpful in a particular game.
> *I actually pulled a Black Lotus from my deck, but it's a CRAP RARE because I have nothing to cast.*

cut scene *(noun)*
A boring scene in a video game where the player is not in control and is forced to sit and watch a CGI or live-action story.
> *I wish I could skip the CUT SCENE. I am sitting alone in the dark on a Friday night to kill monsters, not hear chit chat. I have a world to save here.*

cyberathlete *(noun)*
An "athlete" in the Cyberathlete Professional League, concentrating on competitions that involve computer and video games.
> *I wanted to be a pro basketball player until I realized I wouldn't grow any taller. Now I'm a CYBERATHETE.*

d20 system *(noun)*
The RPG system that uses a twenty-sided die for most rolls. Developed by Wizards of the Coast for Dungeons & Dragons and other RPGs. The d20 system was created so that other companies could make their games compatible with Wizards of the Coast's games.
> *What would a game of craps look like using the D20 SYSTEM?*

dance pad *(noun)*
A flat surface used in dance games such as *Dance Dance Revolution* that is activated by the player using his feet on the pad.
> *My great Aunt Susie lost 100 pounds using the DANCE PAD.*

dark chess *(noun)*

A chess variant where the player is not allowed to see the entire board but can only see his or her own pieces.

DARK CHESS is played by goths while listening to Marilyn Manson while they whine about their parents.

GEEK QUIZ

Nothing is better than watching a cartoon based on your favorite video game. My personal favorite was the *Super Mario Brothers Super Show*. Which video game does *not* have an animated series based on it?

a. *Bomberman*

b. *Legend of Zelda*

c. *Viewtiful Joe*

d. *Crash Bandicoot*

Answer: d

---

dating sim *(noun)*

A genre of video game, usually from Japan, that usually involves a male character whose goal is to sleep with, or sometimes marry, female characters.

Being a player in a DATING SIM is probably less satisfying than it would be in real life, but it makes for good practice.

Deep Blue *(proper noun)*

A chess-playing computer developed by IBM. In 1997, Deep Blue won a match against world champion Gary Kasparov. Deep Blue can evaluate 200 million positions per second.

I don't know why I keep losing on the chess game in my cell phone. It's not DEEP BLUE or anything.

deformable terrain *(noun)*

When terrain in a video game can be destroyed and manipulated.

The most DEFORMABLE TERRAINS in the real world: Afghanistan, Cambodia, New Jersey.

Desert Bus *(proper noun)*
The world's most boring game. A mini game in *Penn and Teller's Smoke and Mirrors*, it requires the player to drive for eight hours from Arizona to Nevada with no pause button and no scenery. The player cannot veer too much or the bus will be towed back to the start in real time. Reaching the destination gives you one point.
Finally, a game that shows us the exciting and fulfilling life of a DESERT BUS driver.

digital pet *(noun)*
Artificial pets on a computer or other device that require completion of such tasks as digital feeding and petting.
A DIGITAL PET is a perfect gift for a man engaged to a love pillow.

dojin soft *(noun)*
Video games made by Japanese consumers based on video games already in the market. Dreamcast is often used because it does not have good copy protection.
Type-Moon was a DOJIN SOFT company that became a successful commercial enterprise.

draft format *(noun)*
A Pokemon card tournament where players don't bring their own decks but instead are given booster packs from which they must create a deck from scratch.
A DRAFT FORMAT shows who has the real Pokemon skills and separates the contenders from the pretenders.

Dragonlance *(proper noun)*
A fictional universe within Dungeons & Dragons, created by Tracy and Laura Hickman, Margaret Weis, and others, that emphasized dragons, which is what TSR felt Dungeons & Dragons was lacking at the time.
The idea for DRAGONLANCE came from the Hickmans while in their car on the way to pick up a job application at TSR. Spoiler alert: They got the job.

dungeon crawl *(noun)*
A scenario in RPGs where the player must navigate through a maze while fighting monsters.
> *Navigating the steam tunnels underneath the university was like being in a DUNGEON CRAWL.*

dungeon master *(noun)*
The person who controls, designs, and officiates an adventure in an RPG such as Dungeons & Dragons. Often shortened to DM.
> *Call in the DUNGEON MASTER. I need discipline!*

Dungeons & Dragons *(proper noun)*
A supremely popular RPG that has been played by over 20 million people. To play, you need a rulebook, polyhedral dice, character sheets, and imagination.
> *You cannot describe to someone what DUNGEONS & DRAGONS is all about. It must be experienced to be appreciated.*

emulator *(noun)*
Using a program on a video game console or computer to imitate and play games from another type of console like a Super Nintendo.
> *Feel like going retro? Get out the EMULATOR.*

end game *(noun)*
The final phase of a chess game when very few pieces are left on the board. Usually each player is trying to promote his or her pawns.
> *I am bringing her back to my room. It is time for the END GAME.*

eroge *(noun)*
A video game in Japan that deals with erotic content and involves anime-style girls. The games can sometimes be erotic RPGs or sex simulators.
> *For someone not interested in RPGs, an EROGE might just be a mind changer.*

evolution *(noun)*
A metamorphosis that occurs in a Pokemon game that increases the character's stats as a result of the character gaining experience.
> *You will experience a geek EVOLUTION after reading this book.*

experience points *(noun)*

A measurement unit in RPGs that shows how far along a character is in a game. Points are awarded for completing quests, reaching goals, and killing enemies. Once a certain amount of points is reached, a player can move to the next experience level.

IRL you get EXPERIENCE POINTS for every date.

farming *(noun)*

In *World of Warcraft*, gold farming is collecting gold and not participating in other elements of the game. It usually involves standing around killing easy opponents. Looked down upon by the game developers and players.

FARMING techniques include skinning all the animals you kill, taking up a gathering profession, and then selling the items at an auction house.

filler *(noun)*

A quick boardgame that is supposed to be completed fast and in a casual manner.

Beer pong may be a FILLER game, but it's all some need to be satisfied.

flawless victory *(noun)*

A win in *Mortal Kombat* where the opponent is killed without the winner losing any life points.

FLAWLESS VICTORIES IRL include Mike Tyson versus Leon Spinks, Germany versus Argentina in the 2010 World Cup, and United States versus Iraq in the first Iraq war.

foam weapon *(noun)*

A weapon that is padded and used in LARP boffer wars, which are role-playing simulated battles.

Were you picking your feet? Yeah, you were sitting on your bed, picking your feet in Poughkeepsie and now you've stuck my partner with your FOAM WEAPON and I'm going to have to listen to him complain about his bowling scores all winter.

fog of war *(noun)*
Used in war strategy games to simulate actual battle conditions by taking away a player's vision of the world and of any opponents.
My friend Lucas sends out overlord observers to every corner of the map in Starcraft *to eliminate the FOG OF WAR.*

Forgotten Realms *(proper noun)*
A campaign in Dungeons & Dragons created by Ed Greenwood in 1967. The world was further popularized after a series of novels by R. A. Salvatore.
Ed Greenwood first began writing stories about FORGOTTEN REALMS as a child before having them published and getting noticed by TSR.

FPS *(noun)*
Short for first-person shooter. A shoot 'em up video game from the point of view of the player. Gained popularity with the release of *Wolfenstein 3D.*
Any FPS where you get to battle a robo-Hitler is worth playing.

frag *(verb)*
To kill someone in a video game, usually in an FPS. The word is derived from the military term for throwing a grenade at a disliked or imcompetent officer.
I've FRAGGED many players in Counter-Strike, *but you have no right to judge me. The horror . . . the horror.*

free-form advancement *(noun)*
A type of leveling up in an RPG based on player choice.
There are so many choices in life. Now with FREE-FORM ADVANCEMENT, there are just as many choices in RPGs. Too bad I always make the wrong choices.

Fridrich Method *(proper noun)*
A common method in solving a Rubik's Cube, devised by Jessica Fridrich, which involves first forming a single-colored cross on one side, and then solving layer by layer.
The fastest speedcubers in the world use the FRIDRICH METHOD.

gambler's fallacy *(noun)*

Based on a gambler's belief that future random events will match past observed random events. But the dice have no memory, and the law of averages only applies over an infinite time period.

It is a GAMBLER'S FALLACY to believe that, because you haven't won in a long time, you are due for a win.

Game of Life *(proper noun)*

A computer game developed by John Conway, it consists of a collection of cells that, based on a set of rules, can live, die, or multiply. It is a cellular automaton. You establish the initial state and put in no further input, then observe its evolution.

IRL I am a powerless loser, but in the GAME OF LIFE I am a winner. Wish it were reversed.

Game Boy *(proper noun)*

A handheld console made by Nintendo that is only 8-bit and black and white but was a very popular precursor to the Game Boy Advance.

Remember getting the first GAME BOY? Now remember why you are losing your hair?

Gamegear *(proper noun)*

A handheld console made by Sega, released after Atari's Lynx and the Turboexpress. Gamegear lost the handheld console war to Game Boy.

GAMEGEARS are really fun for the three minutes you have until the batteries run out.

gamer *(noun)*

An individual who passionately engages regularly in video games or RPGs.

Generation Y is mostly made up of GAMERS, not readers.

game sweatshop *(noun)*

A business venture that involves selling player accounts in MMORPGs like *World of Warcraft* for real money.

If you choose to buy that high-level character off of eBay, it could be from a GAME SWEATSHOP.

GEEK FACT

Interestingly, most video games are also packaged in real sweatshops.

7

ganking *(noun, verb)*
A gang kill. To attack a person with a group in a MMORPG.
Jeanne and her Warcraft *buddies went around GANKING n00bs all day.*

gateway *(noun)*
An introductory boardgame that is played before a player advances to more advanced games.
First I started out with GATEWAY games like checkers. Then I got into the more hardcore stuff like Settlers of Catan.

Gen Con *(proper noun)*
One of the largest gaming conventions in the the United States, held annually in Indianapolis, Indiana. Featured are role-playing games, computer games, miniature wargaming, board games, live-action role-playing games, and collectible card games. There, gamers can also engage in game sessions and tournament play.
At GEN CON, I knew I had met my future wife, when I saw a Dark Elf staring at me across the auditorium.

general game theorem *(noun)*
In every two-player, zero-sum, nonrandom, perfect knowledge game such as checkers, chess, and tic-tac-toe, there exists a perfect strategy guaranteed to at least result in a tie game.
According to the GENERAL GAME THEOREM, a perfect strategy exists for chess, but is too complicated to determine, although computer programmers keep trying.

geocaching *(noun)*
An activity in which players use GPS to locate items hidden in different locations around the world.
Times are so tough lately that many unemployed people have resorted to GEOCACHING to find their next job.

ghetto cosplay *(noun)*

A costume in the cosplay style but done with whatever you have in your house, usually with less than remarkable results.

> *Sorry mom, but I cut up all your clothes to make a GHETTO COSPLAY outfit. I hope you didn't need them.*

Ghettopoly *(proper noun)*

A Monopoly-type game based upon life in the ghetto.

> *Pieces in GHETTOPOLY include a prostitute, a pimp, a crack rock, and a pair of fuzzy dice.*

gimped *(noun)*

A character or item that is lacking in quality or very weak.

> *Bring out the GIMPED!*

glitching *(noun)*

The video game practice of finding glitches in a game and then exploiting them.

> *If you find your character floating in the middle of a wall, then you are GLITCHING.*

G-Man *(proper noun)*

A mysterious and iconic character in the computer game *Half-Life* that appears often to observe and interact with the player, although who he works for is a secret.

> *The G-MAN is like the Cigarette Smoking Man in* The X-Files.

Go *(proper noun)*

An ancient Chinese board game that originated around 2,500 years ago that is simple in its rules but complex in strategy.

> *Confucius would be totally pwned if he ever played me at GO.*

God mode *(noun)*

When a player in a video game is invincible.

> *GOD MODE is usually attained by a star in* Mario Brothers *or by using a cheat code.*

GoldenEye 007 *(proper noun)*

A game on the Nintendo 64 that was based on the James Bond movie and became one of the most popular multiplayer games in history, entertaining drunk college students across the country.

I was feared among my friends for my deadly aim in GOLDENEYE 007.

Goob *(noun)*

A person who is obsessed with video and computer gaming and makes it a central part of his or her life.

I'm about to rage quit because some gaming GOOB keeps fragging me.

goomba *(noun)*

1. Basic enemy in *Super Mario Brothers,* brown in color, and designed like a shitake mushroom. 2. A person who is a moron.

Like in Super Mario Brothers, *real life GOOMBAS are enemies: enemies of humanity!*

grand strategy wargame *(noun)*

A game that deals with real-life macro elements such as the resources and politics of a nation at war; examples include *Risk* and *Diplomacy.*

If the war in Afghanistan was a GRAND STRATEGY WARGAME, we'd be losing our ass.

griefer *(noun)*

A player in a multiplayer online game whose sole purpose is to annoy and disrupt others.

Stop annoying me! You are being a total GRIEFER right now.

grinding *(noun)*

In a video game, usually an RPG, the engagement in repetitive behavior to achieve some goal.

GRINDING is similar to reality, and, therefore, not fun.

Grue *(proper noun)*

A monster that exists in the darkness, used in Jack Vance's *Dying Earth* books, as well as in the computer game *Zork*. The Grue was created to stop or limit what a player could do in an unlit area and force the player into the light to solve puzzles.

I am not afraid of the dark. It's the GRUE I'm worried about.

guess the verb *(noun)*

A type of game where the player types out commands for the character. There are so many options that the player ends up trying every combination of verb and item.

> *When you GUESS THE VERB in* Leisure Suit Larry, *it is usually, "Walk to bar, order drink, piss off waitress."*

guild *(noun)*

Also called a clan; a group of people in an online video game that play together.

> *I've been GUILD leader for two years and it has been a peaceful reign, but there are murmurs of revolt that I must strike down with an iron fist.*

GURPS *(proper noun)*

Short for generic universal role-playing system. A general system that is adaptable to whatever role-playing game universe the player desires.

> *I once made a GURPS game to emulate my own life, then I realized that except for role-playing games, I really have no life.*

hack and slash *(noun)*

A video game or RPG that has a lot of fighting and hand-to-hand combat, such as *Diablo.*

> *Experts disagree on whether HACK AND SLASH video games cause aggressive behavior or relieve it.*

hadouken *(noun)*

An attack used by Ryu and Ken in *Street Fighter* games. Translated from Japanese as "wave motion fist" or "surge fist," it allows characters to shoot a burst of energy, known as a "chi blast," from their hands.

> *If your opponent has the reach advantage, use the HADOUKEN.*

headshot *(noun)*

In first-person shooters when a player is killed immediately by being hit in the head with a single bullet.

> *Jim trained every day for hours until he was a cold-blooded killer, able to kill other players without remorse. He was quick and clean, and used only a single HEADSHOT to end another's virtual life.*

healbot *(noun)*
A character in an RPG that heals other players but doesn't do much else.
Many clerics in AD&D were little more than pious HEALBOTS.

HMD *(noun)*
Short for head-mounted display. An electronic headset and screen used in 3D virtual reality games.
Hopefully, in the future, HMD wont be necessary, and contact lenses with projected images will be all that are needed.

homebrew *(noun)*
Video games that are made by consumers, usually for older consoles.
Due to a flaw in its embedded software, the Sega Dreamcast is very popular for HOMEBREW games; actually more popular than it is for professionally produced games.

GEEK QUIZ

It seems like arcade games have been around forever and have come so far, as they now have arcade games using cockpits and virtual reality head sets. What is the name of the first coin-operated arcade game?

a. Galaxy Game

b. Pong

c. Tennis

d. Space Brohemes

Answer: a

Hot Coffee *(proper noun)*
A mod in *Grand Theft Auto: San Andreas* that was controversial because it portrayed the main character having sex with his girlfriend, who had invited him over for coffee.
Even Hillary Clinton knew about the HOT COFFEE mod, and suggested new regulations be placed on video games. Rumor has it that she found out about the game while catching hubby Bill using the mod.

HP *(noun)*
Short for hit points. When you run out of these, you are dead.
My grandmother ran out of HIT POINTS a few months ago.

HUD *(noun)*
Short for heads-up display. The user interface in a video game that overlays information on the screen, including ammo, life, maps, or other useful data.
HUD was first developed by the military.

hunt the pixel *(noun)*
Clues in adventure games that are very hard to find because they are only the size of a few pixels.
Playing The Secret of Monkey Island *often turned into a game of HUNT THE PIXEL.*

imaginary number *(noun)*
An imaginary number uses i, where i equals the square root of -1. The number represented by i is said to be imaginary because -1 does not have a square root in the real number system. Adding an imaginary number to a real number forms a complex number in the form $a + bi$. Complex numbers, particulary as used in the quaternion number system, are extremely useful in solving rotation and orientation problems in 3-D computer-generated animation.
It takes a lot of imagination to comprehend IMAGINARY NUMBERS.

GEEK QUIZ

Dungeons & Dragons was published by TSR in 1974 and was influenced by mythology, fantasy fiction, and pulp fiction. Dungeons & Dragons was created by:

a. Andy Novitz & Erik Larson

b. Gary Gygax & Dave Arneson

c. Max Sydney & Jean Stanford

d. Al Mxyzptlk & Frank Orvitz

Answer: b

---

incapped *(adjective)*
Describes an RPG character that has fallen but is not dead.
Help, I'm INCAPPED and I cant get up.

instagib *(noun)*
In a special game mode in a video game, a weapon that can kill an enemy in one hit. As seen in *Quake* and *Unreal*.
The mech in District 9 *had a similar one-shot, one-kill INSTAGIB weapon.*

instance dungeon *(noun)*
In an MMORPG, a new dungeon or area that is created for each party that enters it so that different parties don't run into each other and compete for kills or loot. It gives each party a fresh dungeon.
This INSTANCE DUNGEON is giving me déjà vu.

insult swordfighting *(noun)*
From the *Monkey Island* computer games, where a swordfight is won by defeating an opponent using insults.
I see you are well-versed in INSULT SWORDFIGHTING. I fight like a dairy farmer? How appropriate. You fight like a cow.

janky *(adjective)*
Describes a deck in Magic: The Gathering that looks crappy.
Don't bring that JANKY deck around my deck or else it will be pwned.

GEEK FACT

Geek Rant
Ever notice that the Johns and Johnnies of the world are out of control?
John is violent: Johnny get your gun
John is tardy: Johnny come lately
John is a gangster: Johnny Dangerously
John is lonesome: Johnny is a john
No wonder John's girlfriend left him a "Dear John" letter.

Johnny *(proper noun)*
A player who wins a battle or quest in an RPG game in a cool or dramatic way.
> *The only JOHNNY I know got his butt kicked in* The Karate Kid, *which was not a cool win. Put him in a body bag, Johnny, yeah!*

Jumpman *(proper noun)*
The Nintendo character Mario's original name as used in the 1981 game *Donkey Kong*. Donkey Kong is actually Jumpman's pet who was mistreated and, for revenge, kidnapped his girlfriend, the Lady.
> *In the ghetto, you always have to watch out for the JUMPMAN— especially if you have a brand-new pair of expensive sneakers.*

kill stealing *(noun)*
The act of stealing a kill from a player in a video game usually by coming in at the last moment to deliver the coup de grâce.
> *There is nothing more satisfying than KILL STEALING because so little work is involved.*

kiting *(noun)*
In an RPG, firing at an enemy from a distance using a projectile weapon.
> *KITING is the only option for a sorcerer who cannot fight in hand-to-hand combat with much success.*

Konami code *(noun)*
A cheat code that appears in many Konami games and is famously in the NES game *Contra*: Up, Up, Down, Down, Left, Right, Left, Right, B, A.
> *Just to be safe, try the KONAMI CODE on every game you play.*

lag *(noun)*
Slowed gameplay, sometimes even a frozen screen, usually due to a bad Internet connection. Really annoying.
> *There is no worse LAG than having the screen freeze when you are at a critical level!*

lame duck *(noun)*
A player in a game or video game that has no chance of winning.
> *In any game I play, every other player is a LAME DUCK.*

LAN *(noun)*

Short for local area network; a system, usually limited to one building, to link computers to share data, programs, and printers; the most common connections are Ethernet and wi-fi. LANs were seen as early as the 1970s in laboratories and universities such as the Lawrence Radiation Laboratory. LANs are heavily used in playing multiplayer computer games at houses, dorms, and LAN gaming centers.

Setting up a LAN system to play Starcraft *with my friends taught me a lot about computers.*

LAN party *(noun)*

When a group of people get together to play a multiplayer game such as *Starcraft* or *Counter-Strike* over a LAN.

Our raging LAN PARTY was broken up by the cops last night. Apparently, the Warcraft *music was too loud and the neighbors complained.*

LARP *(noun)*

Short for live-action role-playing game. A role-playing game where the players dress up as their characters and act out virtual events in real life. An example of a LARP would be to engage in a fake medieval battle while dressed as a wizard or as an ancient infantryman.

Hey guys, we got this Elizabethan-era LARP happening at the park today. You guys got any spare garter belts?

level-based progression *(noun)*

A type of leveling up in an RPG based on experience points.

LEVEL-BASED PROGRESSION is used in games such as Dungeons & Dragons. Once you level up, you obtain superior abilities and traits.

light gun *(noun)*

A gun used in a video game, such as *Duck Hunt* on the NES. It works by blacking out the screen when the trigger is pressed, and a diode starts receiving a signal. The screen turns white and then the system can determine where the gun is aimed.

When it comes to arcade LIGHT GUNS, I am a sharpshooter in The House of the Dead *and* Area 51.

GEEK QUIZ

Comic cons are not just for those who want to buy comics. They are now a gathering for all things geek, and a lot of money is spent to make sure people are entertained. What is the name of the real-life walk-through dungeon role-playing game at Gen Con?

a. True Dungeon

b. Gnome Quest

c. Dungeon Slayer

d. Magic & Mystics

Answer: a

looting *(noun)*
Taking money or equipment from a dead body in a video game.

LOOTING is also used to denote one of the most popular weekend activities in downtown Baghdad.

Lord British *(proper noun)*
The ruler of Britannia in the *Ultima* computer game series. Also the near indestructible in-game persona of game creator Richard Garriott. The first *Ultima* computer game was released in 1980. It is considered one of the first computer RPGs.

LORD BRITISH was once killed during a meeting when he forgot to turn on his immortality, causing the game moderators to kill everyone in the town meeting.

Magic missile *(proper noun)*
A famous spell from Dungeons & Dragons where energy is shot from one's fingertips.

I cast MAGIC MISSILE at the darkness!

magic satchel *(noun)*
The ability of a player to carry many more items than is physically possible, which must be due to some sort of magic satchel.

The MAGIC SATCHEL is the game equivalent of a circus clown car.

Magic: The Gathering *(proper noun)*
A card game where players collect and assemble decks containing mana, spells, items, and monsters, and compete against each other in battles.
I always destroyed Nick and Jose at MAGIC: THE GATHERING with so many fireballs and forks (which double the damage), that it must have been embarrassing for them.

7

GEEK QUIZ

Getting to the top of the high score list in a video game is a great accomplishment and gives a gamer true geek cred. But when did it all begin? The first electronic game that included a list of the highest scores was:

a. Sea Wolf

b. Star Fire

c. Asteroids

d. Battle for Uranus

Answer: b

---

mana *(noun)*
A magical unit that must be collected to cast a spell or perform a magical act. Mana or its derivatives are used extensively in RPGs, video games, and card games such as Magic: The Gathering.
I never have enough MANA to cast my Shivan Dragon!

Mario Kart *(proper noun)*
A racing game starring Mario originally on the Super Nintendo in 1992, and now with multiple versions on different platforms.
With so many versions of MARIO KART, there are many Rainbow Roads from which to fall.

Master Chief *(proper noun)*
The hero of the *Halo* game series. He is a cyborg soldier that always wears a helmet and armor.
Because of a bad case of acne, the MASTER CHIEF covered his face with a mask.

7

meat shield *(noun)*

A character in an RPG who is at the front of the attack and can withstand more damage than the rest of the party.

> *MEAT SHIELDS take the most hits and are put in the most dangerous situations. They are like the Marines of the video game world.*

metagaming *(noun)*

To play a game using knowledge not found within the game, such as the mathematics of an RPG or the intentions of the gamemaster.

> *METAGAMING is similar to insider trading in the stock market and is frowned upon.*

metaplot *(noun)*

The large story arc of an RPG.

> *The "Time of Troubles" METAPLOT for* Forgotten Realms *involved gods that walk the world in mortal form.*

miniature wargaming *(noun)*

A genre of game played with miniature figurines that focuses on war strategies and tactics.

> *H. G. Wells is the founder of MINIATURE WARGAMING, producing "Little Wars" in 1913.*

minimax game theorem *(noun)*

A theorem that states that if all players in a game use the most rational strategy, the resulting outcome of the game will be predictable.

> *MINIMAX GAME THEOREM doesn't work for the stock market because investors' decisions are affected by emotions like fear and greed. Mostly greed.*

Ms Pac-Man *(proper noun)*

The first female video game character, she starred in the game Ms Pac-Man, a game created by hackers who copied the original Pac-Man game without authorization. The game was purchased by Midway games and became a success.

> *Pepper is the name of MS PAC-MAN in the* Pac-Man *animated series from the 1980s.*

MissingNo. *(proper noun)*
A glitch Pokemon creature in the video game *Pokemon Red and Blue* that was accidentally named MissingNo. because "missing number" was used by the programmers as a placeholder for missing data.
Many fans still believe that MISSINGNO. was done purposely, which has led to scientific studies on the sociological issues of fandom.

M-m-m-monster kill *(phrase)*
Making 6 kills in a short time period in the game *Unreal*.
The greatest sound in the world is hearing a M-M-M-MONSTER KILL.

MMORPG *(noun)*
Short for massive multiplayer online role-playing game. Examples include *World of Warcraft*, *Ultima Online*, and *Warhammer Online*.
Not to be confused with MMORPG: Mongrels from Mongolia online racquetball player group, or MMORPG: massive monkeys online radio program group.

GEEK FACT

Geek Contest
Send in your own MMORPG funny acronym to us at: *www.Funny AcronymⓐWeWillNeverReadThis.org*
We'll pick a winner. FYI—the winner gets NADA . . . not an acronym. Just means you don't get anything.

mod *(noun)*
A module or modification, usually to a computer game. The *Elder Scrolls* series is famous for allowing players to add modifications, including new creatures, abilities, and quests.
I added so many MODs to Morrowind *that my character was able to teleport, fly anywhere, and kill anyone with one hit.*

mod trade *(noun)*

An online trade using Pokemon or Magic: The Gathering cards where the players use a website moderator to ensure that a trade is fair. Necessary because the players don't trust each other.

I should have used a MOD TRADE before I gave up my Dual Land for a Murk Dweller.

module *(noun)*

An adventure in AD&D or an RPG sold as a separate item.

I'd like to buy the MODULE where I am a spy on Mars.

Monster Manual *(proper noun)*

A bestiary of monsters for Dungeons & Dragons.

Excerpt from the MONSTER MANUAL: Vampires—Emo high school student that is so, like, emo.

monster player kill *(noun)*

A strategy used in MMORPGs where a player lures a monster into harming and killing other players to take out the competition.

MONSTER PLAYER KILL is a great and effective form of strategery.

MUD *(noun)*

Short for multi-user dungeon. A real-time computer virtual reality RPG that players log into to explore the environment and interact with other players.

MUDS are the ancestors of games like World of Warcraft.

mulligan *(noun)*

The redoing of a move in a game. In *Magic: The Gathering*, a player can call a mulligan and redraw the initial draw if the cards are unsatisfactory.

Why couldn't I have a MULLIGAN after I crashed my car into the garage door?

munchkin *(noun)*

A player in an RPG or online game that wants to win and be competitive no matter how much it detracts from the other player's enjoyment.

A MUNCHKIN just killed his own teammate because he was doing better than him. Sociopath.

nerf *(verb)*, Nerf *(noun)*
1. To decrease or soften an element in a game such as a feature that is too powerful. 2. A toy brand that uses foam-like material. It began as a Nerf Ball and evolved into weapons such as the Nerf Blaster.

The swords in Ultima Online *were NERFED and made less powerful —so much so that players complained it was like they were hitting each other with Nerf bats.*

net deck *(noun)*
A *Magic: The Gathering* or *Pokemon* deck that is identical to a proven deck suggested on the Internet.

Dude, you can't brag about your deck like you built it when it's just a NET DECK.

ninja *(noun)*
In *World of Warcraft*, a player who steals items that are undeserved.

NINJA attack swiftly, steal the wooden armor, and then disappear into shadow without a trace.

n00b *(noun)*
A newbie or new player in a game who obviously doesn't know what he or she is doing.

I don't want OgReDeStRoYeR-711 on my team, he is a total N00B.

non-zero-sum game *(noun)*
A game in which both or multiple players can win or lose, where there is no fixed total value so that one player's win doesn't correspond to another player's loss. Poker is a zero-sum game because any chip or dollar amount won by one player means another player lost that amount.

Chicken is an example of a NON-ZERO-SUM GAME—if one swerves, the other wins; if both swerve, no one wins, but both survive. If neither survives, both lose, so the ideal strategy is to swerve.

Noob Saibot *(proper noun)*
A secret character in *Mortal Kombat* that appears after the player has won fifty games in a row.

NOOB SAIBOT, Scorpion, Sub-Zero, and Smoke all must shop at the same department store because they all look the same.

Norrath *(proper noun)*
The fictional fantasy world that exists in *Everquest*, a 3D MMORPG released in 1999.

NORRATH is made up of the Surface world, the Underfoot, and the Overrealm.

NPC *(noun)*
Short for nonplayer character. Characters in an RPG or video game that are controlled by the gamemaster or the game itself.

Most people I encounter during the day are NPCs.

Nuclear launch detected *(phrase)*
A quote from a ghost in *Starcraft* when a nuclear weapon is used.

That burrito isn't sitting well. I'm about to let off a big one. NUCLEAR LAUNCH DETECTED.

nuts draw *(noun)*
When a player in *Magic: The Gathering* or *Pokemon* draws his best seven cards on his first draw.

I had the best NUTS DRAW ever and was able to bring out my favorite card, the Mox Emerald, giving me one more green mana.

n'wah *(noun)*
A derogatory term used in the computer game *Morrowind* that means "foreigner."

Get your filthy hands off me, you damn dirty N'WAH.

OD&D *(proper noun)*
Short for Original Dungeons & Dragons. Published in 1974 by TSR, Inc. It was a much simpler game, with only three character classes and four races. The precursor to Advanced Dungeons & Dragons.

OD&D is the OG of RPGs.

otome *(noun)*
A type of video game made for girls where the goal of the player is to make one of several boy characters fall in love with her character.

An OTOME is an interactive version of The Bachelorette.

GEEK QUIZ

Monopoly is one of the most popular games of all time, and players debate which properties should be purchased. What is the most commonly landed-upon property in the game, excluding the Jail?

a. Illinois Avenue

b. Park Place

c. Tennessee Avenue

d. Saint Charles Place

Answer: a

outro *(noun)*

The ending of a computer game, usually an animation or movie that is the reward to the player for finishing the game.

> *The worst OUTRO was for* Rampage *on the Nintendo. After destroying dozens of cities as Godzilla for hours and hours, all it said was, "Congratulations."*

overextend *(verb)*

In Pokemon, to use too many of one kind of card, such as monsters, leaving the player exposed to other forms of attack.

> *I am going to OVEREXTEND my deck because I think it will be worth it in the short run.*

overworld *(noun)*

The world map in a video game that is used to maneuver one's way around the world of the game.

> *Everyone has an OVERWORLD map that they love. Mine would be the map of Skara Brae from* The Bard's Tale, *an awesome RPG game from 1985 that I played as a kid.*

"Pac-Man Fever" *(proper noun)*

Song from the 1980s that was a hit created by Buckner & Garcia based on the game Pac-Man.

> *The follow up to "PAC-MAN FEVER" was the less successful "Do the Donkey Kong."*

GEEK QUIZ

What types of numbers are particularly useful in performing the mathematical calculations necessary for the 3D animation used in computer and video games?

a. Imaginary numbers

b. Euclidean numbers

c. Irrational numbers

d. Astleford numbers

Answer: a

parallax scrolling *(noun)*

A technique used in video games since 1982 and in animation since the 1940s where the background moves slower than the foreground, making the environment appear more in-depth.

Anyone who has played a video game in the 1980s and 1990s knows what PARALLAX SCROLLING looks like.

PARS *(proper noun)*

Short for PAPA Advanced Rating System. PAPA stands for professional amateur pinball association. A math-intensive system for rating pinball players. PARS uses the Glicko rating system, which is similar to the Elo rating system, which are both used in rating chess players.

My friends laugh at me now. But one day I'll have a top PARS rating, they'll see!

perks *(noun)*

Special abilities that a player can add to his or her character in an RPG or video game.

Examples of PERKS: super speed, super strength, and financial independence.

perma death *(noun)*

When a character in a video game is permanently dead and there is no resurrection or "to be continued."

My grandfather experienced a PERMA DEATH a few years ago.

persistent world *(noun)*

In a computer game, a world that continues to exist even when the player is not hooked in. Persistent worlds include *Second Life* and *World of Warcraft*.

How do we know that the world we live in is a PERSISTENT WORLD and doesn't disappear when we shut our eyes.

Petrus Method *(proper noun)*

A method used to solve a Rubik's Cube, devised by Lars Petrus, a champion speedcuber. This method alters the layer by layer approach of the Fridrich Method, and involves solving the cube beginning from one corner.

Using the PETRUS METHOD, Lars Petrus once solved a Rubik's cube in 13.60 seconds.

pew pew *(noun)*

The sound of a laser in video games and in sci-fi movies, used in a joking manner by gamers and online.

PEW PEW is a good example of onomatopoeia.

pixel art *(noun)*

A type of art using raster graphics or bitmap graphics where the 2D image is designed at the pixel level. Pixel art was seen in early video and computer games.

We all love the retro look of PIXEL ART compared to the soulless capitalist 3D art that is so prevalent in modern times.

poaching *(noun)*

In a video game, to stay in the same area to collect a particular item, such as the body armor in *GoldenEye 007*.

The only reason Joel won so much was because he kept POACHING the rocket launcher.

pogs *(noun)*

Circular collectible playing pieces played in a game that was created in Hawaii in the 1920s and popular in the 1990s.

My father had a terrible POGS addiction. We never had any food, but sometimes he'd come home with a truckload of pogs.

7

point and click *(noun)*

An old-school type of computer adventure game that involved the player leading a character through an imaginary world using the mouse to click on objects and actions. An example is the *Monkey Island* series and many other LucasArts games.

POINT AND CLICK games are making a comeback, as shown by the new Monkey Island *games, including the special edition of* Monkey Island 2.

Poke Ball *(proper noun)*

A spherical device that is used to capture Pokemon creatures and store them. They are converted to energy once inside the ball and released when the ball is thrown when fighting other Pokemon.

A bright light emitted from my POKE BALL and released Pikachu to fight Charizard.

Pokedex *(proper noun)*

An encyclopedia that describes all of the characters in the Pokemon universe.

The POKEDEX tells me that Pikachu has electric powers and can shoot lightning bolts.

Pokemon Professor *(proper noun)*

An official in a Pokemon tournament that has passed a test and is now responsible for regulating the tournament.

Kissing up to a POKEMON PROFESSOR won't help you win a game.

polyhedral dice *(noun)*

A type of multisided dice used in RPG games with twenty, twelve, ten, or eight sides. They are used to randomly determine the outcome of events and how much damage a character or item inflicts on an opponent.

You want to mess with me? Roll the POLYHEDRAL DICE and take your chances, because I eat breakfast 300 yards away from 4,000 Cubans who are trained to kill me. So don't think for a second you can come down here, flash some POLYHEDRAL DICE, and make me nervous.

GEEK QUIZ

World of Warcraft has a large following as well as a diverse and complex world filled with many heroes and monsters. What are *not* creatures that exist in the MMORPG *World of Warcraft*?

a. Naga

b. Meglar

c. Murloc

d. Tauren

Power Glove *(proper noun)*
An NES special controller worn like a glove but very difficult to use. Short lived.

"I love the POWER GLOVE, its so bad!" –Bully in the movie The Wizard.

powerleveling *(noun)*
The attainment of a high level in an RPG using different strategies that deviate from the standard path.

POWERLEVELING is similar to taking steroids.

power-ups *(noun)*
Items that grant special abilities in a video game. One type of power up is a Pac-Man power pellet.

After a slow morning, Warren grabbed a Redbull for a POWER-UP.

Prisoner's Dilemma *(proper noun)*
A famous non-zero-sum strategy game. In the game, two suspects are arrested. During the police interrogation, each is offered the same plea bargain. If one suspect informs on the other, he can go free, but the other suspect will get five years in jail. If both prisoners inform on each other, they will both get three years. But if neither cooperates, they will both walk away free. What should they do?

The game show Friend or Foe *put the players into a PRISONER'S DILEMMA situation.*

proxy (noun)
A replacement for a card in a Magic: The Gathering or Pokemon card game where a player writes the name of a card on a slip of paper and uses it instead of the real thing. Used to test how a card works in a deck before making a purchase.

An entire deck of PROXIES is probably not allowed.

pwned (adjective)
To be dominated by another player in an online game. Meant to be "owned," but spelled "pwned" to reflect a common typo made in online games.

Every guy that shows up on To Catch a Predator *gets PWNED by Chris Hansen.*

Quake Done Quick (proper noun)
A series of popular online videos that show levels in the first-person shooter *Quake* being completed as fast as possible using various tricks and short cuts.

QUAKE DONE QUICK is a video game version of speedcubing.

ragdoll physics (noun)
The animation used for computer and video game characters that have been killed so that they fall in a way that mimics Newtonian physics. For example, the use of ragdoll physics allows for the weight and position of a body to determine whether a character slumped over a cliff will fall over the ledge.

The first game to use RAGDOLL PHYSICS was Jurassic Park: Trespasser.

rage quit (verb)
To quit a video game in frustration in a dramatic and often amusing act of rage that usually involves throwing the controller or smashing the keyboard.

A huge nerd fight erupted after one of the players RAGE QUIT.

raid (noun)
A group venture where many players in an MMORPG team up and contribute in different ways to fight a difficult boss and collect the loot after the victory.

During a RAID, my only purpose is to heal other players. I'm a lover not a fighter.

7

redemption game *(noun)*
An arcade game that gives out tickets for the amount of points scored. The tickets can be turned in for prizes. Examples are skeeball and mini-basketball.

I had to win 10,000 REDEMPTION GAME tickets just to get a stuffed animal.

regen kill *(verb)*
In a video game, to wait in an area where other players regenerate so that you can kill them right after they regenerate. Also known as "spawn killing."

If you REGEN KILL, then you are a cheap bastard and deserve to be ganked.

remorting *(noun)*
In an RPG, when a character reaches a certain level and has an option of restarting with a new version of his character.

City of Heroes *used REMORTING, allowing a new character class to be available once the player hit a certain level.*

ROM hacking *(noun)*
When a person hacks into a ROM image of a video game to alter the game.

ROM HACKING can give Mario an afro but it can't get the Princess to put out.

RPG *(noun)*
Short for role-playing game. RPGs have evolved from using only pen and paper, to LARPS, where players act out their roles, to massive online RPGs such as *World of Warcraft*.

RPGs can be traced back to "creative history" games played by historical reenactment groups in the 1960s as well as to war games played by Prussian officers in the nineteenth century.

replay value *(noun)*
Replayability; how many times a video game can be played over and over again before the player gets sick of it.

Things that have little or no REPLAY VALUE are suicide and the movie Gigli..

rez *(verb)*

To create an object, such as a shirt or a chair, in the computer simulation *Second Life*. A rezday is the day that a Resident's account is created.

> *We REZZED a line of cosplay fashion that sold for a lot of money on* Second Life.

sandbagging *(noun)*

A strategy used in games (mainly in Texas Hold'em) by playing a hand passively in the hopes of inducing your opponents to bet more and call your bluff. Sandbagging is a common strategy in many sports including using the fake-injured chicken leg in football to cause your opponents to misjudge your speed.

> *Both the Dread Pirate Roberts and Inigo Montoya engaged in SANDBAGGING in their famous duel in* The Princess Bride.

sandbox gameplay *(noun)*

A video game that gives the player multiple options and an expansive world that is highly interactive, giving lots of freedom. Examples are *Grand Theft Auto* and *The Elder Scrolls* series.

> *SANDBOX GAMEPLAY is closer to reality than most games.*

saving throw *(noun)*

A throw of the dice in an RPG that will determine the outcome of a spell or effectiveness of an item used against an opponent.

> *This SAVING THROW will determine whether Bob the troll can safely jump over the mud puddle.*

scaling *(verb)*

Using an electronic scale to weigh a pack of cards such as Yu-Gi-Oh! to tell whether it has a rare card in it, because the rare cards have a slightly different weight.

> *If I worked at a comic store I would start SCALING the booster packs immediately.*

SCUMM *(proper noun)*

Computer game engine used by LucasArts for games such as *Maniac Mansion* and *Monkey Island*. It gives the player only a few options such as "Push," "Pull," and "Look at."

> *The SCUMM engine did not include options for "Sleep," "Give Up and Go Home," or "Sit in Cubicle for Eight Hours."*

Settlers of Catan *(proper noun)*
A hugely popular multi-player board game originating in Germany that has been called one of the greatest games ever created because every time the game is played it is a new experience and because so much strategy is necessary. Settlers of Catan won the Spiel de Jahres (Game of the Year) in 1995.

The original name, "Pure-Blooded Aryan Settlers," was changed for marketing purposes to SETTLERS OF CATAN.

GEEK FACT

Geeks have been playing games for centuries. The oldest board game is Senet, from 3500 BC, played in Egypt. Patolli was played in ancient South America, and a backgammon board was found in Iran dating to 3000 BC. Additionally, the predecessors of chess date back to the sixth century in India, whereas the modern version is from fifteenth century Europe.

shoryuken *(noun)*
An attack used by Ryu and Ken in *Street Fighter* games. Translated from Japanese as "rising dragon fist," it allows the character to use an uppercut to strike an enemy in the air.

HADOUKEN. HADOUKEN. SHORYUKEN!

side scroller *(noun)*
A type of platform video game where the character is shown in a 2D environment with the ability to jump, shoot, and collect items. Examples include *Super Mario Brothers* and *Sonic the Hedgehog*.

The first SIDE SCROLLER was Defender, which was released in 1980.

GEEK FACT

Geek Food for Thought
In Chinese and Hebrew, one reads from right to left, not left to right. Do Chinese and Israelis find it awkward to play a side scroller that moves from left to right?

simming *(noun)*

A text-based game that is played online, usually in chat rooms or forums.
SIMMING is most popular with Star Trek, Star Wars, *and* Stargate *universes.*

skill-based progression *(noun)*

A type of leveling up in an RPG based on a character's statistics. The more you use a skill, the better you get at it.
SKILL-BASED PROGRESSION is used in Final Fantasy 14.

slot machine conditioning mechanisms *(noun)*

Offer of a big win to entice people to play. Includes having frequent near wins plus bells, whistles, and flashing lights showing winners on nearby machines. In other words, turn the players into rats in a maze with no cheese at the end.
Despite the SLOT MACHINE CONDITIONING MECHANISMS, Marsha continues to beat the House time and time again.

Sneasel *(proper noun)*

A Pokemon trading card that was banned because it was too powerful in tournaments. It had the ability to cause 120 points of damage in one turn, leading most Sneasel-holding players to victory.
The word SNEASEL is a combination of the words "sneaky" and "weasel."

spawning *(noun)*

Having one's character recreated or regenerated after death in a video or computer game.
SPAWNING would be a great concept for real life.

speedball *(noun)*

A paintball game that occurs in an area surrounded by man-made barriers and bunkers.
I've built a SPEEDBALL gaming field filled with a series of obstacles and deadly traps.

speedcubing *(noun)*
To try and solve a Rubik's Cube in the shortest time possible. If you enter a World Cube Association competition, make sure to lubricate the cube and use the Fridrich or Petrus methods.
Yo, I challenge you to a SPEEDCUBING battle right now, dawg.

Spiel de Jahres *(proper noun)*
A prestigious German award for board and card games, where board games are usually made to avoid conflict because violence in games is taboo there.
Not a surprise that the SPIEL DE JAHRES takes place in Germany. After all, who hates violence more than the Germans?

sprite *(noun)*
A 2D image created using pixel illustration tools that appeared in early computer games.
Z SPRITES were used in Kings Quest VI, *which are sprites in a 3D environment.*

squishy *(noun)*
In a computer game such as *World of Warcraft,* a priest, mage, warlock, or any character that wears clothing but no armor.
Due to my being an overweight kid, my nickname in junior high was SQUISHY. Sad, huh?

Starcade *(proper noun)*
A game show involving arcade games that ran in the early 1980s.
Games played in STARCADE included Dragon's Lair *and* Star Wars.

Stratego *(proper noun)*
A two-player board game with forty pieces representing soldiers and officers. The object is to capture the flag. The game is so popular that people have even named their children after the game.
My friends and I often played the Marvel Comics version of STRATEGO.

Stump Joke *(proper noun)*
In the *Secret of Monkey Island,* a joke programmers put in the game in which when a player finds a stump, he is told to insert various discs that don't exist—"disc 23, 47, 114"—and then told he will have to skip that part of the game.
The STUMP JOKE prompted many calls to the game makers and caused much confusion and anger.

tabletop RPG *(noun)*
An RPG played by a group of people where the in-game actions are described and executed orally, and events are recorded and determined using paper and dice, all of which is led by a gamemaster.
The largest publisher of TABLETOP RPGS is Wizards of the Coast.

tactical event *(noun)*
An unscripted historical reenactment that is performed realistically, with both sides trying to defeat the other using strategies and tactics.
My dorm mate George was the Napoleon of TACTICAL EVENTS.

tech *(noun)*
A type of Pokemon card that is placed in a deck specifically to combat certain threats. An important part of a player's strategy.
I use my Dewgong TECH CARD to stop fire and water decks.

tell *(noun)*
In card games, a mannerism or body language that a player displays that reveals the true strength of his or her hand.
Le Chiffre's TELL in the movie Casino Royale *is that he weeps blood when he gets nervous.*

tetromino *(noun)*
A shape that is made of four squares in different configurations. Used in the game *Tetris.*
If the trash in my room was shaped like TETROMINO, it would be much easier to clean.

text-based game *(noun)*
A computer adventure game using text only, popular in the 1970s and 1980s.
Why go to Studio 54 when you can have just as much fun playing a TEXT-BASED GAME in the comfort of your own home?

ThacO *(noun)*
An acronym for "to hit Armor Class 0." The ability of a Dungeons & Dragons character to strike another character. The lowest roll on a die.

THAC0 was taken out of the newer editions of Dungeons & Dragons to the dismay of many players.

thrash *(verb)*
To click all over a screen with a mouse while playing a video game to find something relevant to gameplay. A necessary action in games such as *Myst* or LucasArts games like *The Secret of Monkey Island.*

I am going to THRASH tonight, brah! No, I don't mean have a party and trash a hotel room. I mean I am going to click my mouse a lot all over a screen.

timing attack *(noun)*
An attack in *Starcraft* that is done before the opponent can build up a proper defense. It requires good scouting.

By constantly putting pressure on an opponent using TIMING ATTACKS, he was able to create an expansion base without being under enemy fire.

toasty *(phrase)*
A high-pitched exclamation of "Toasty!" emitted in *Mortal Kombat* that was triggered by an uppercut, accompanied by an image of one of the creative team

Instead of TOASTY, in Mortal Kombat 3, *Sub-Zero's freeze triggers a "Frosty!"*

top decking *(noun)*
When a player of a card game such as *Magic: The Gathering* or *Yu-Gi-Oh!* has no more cards in his hand and must draw from the top of the deck. Top decking makes cheating possible because a player can place a desired card on the top of the deck after shuffling. That is why cutting the deck after shuffling is necessary.

One of our friends was caught TOP DECKING. Shortly thereafter, he mysteriously disappeared, never to be seen again. Catch my drift?

Triforce *(proper noun)*

A relic in the *Zelda* games that is made of three triangles, which represent Golden Goddesses. When the Triforce is brought together, the user can make any wish he or she wants.

TRIFORCE resembles a Sierpinski triangle, which is a type of fractal.

twinking *(verb)*

Leveling up very fast in an RPG using the resources of a higher-level character.

Even if you like TWINKING, never refer to yourself as a twink. It has a totally different connotation.

unwinnable *(adjective)*

Describes a computer game or text adventure becomes impossible to win. In the *Hitchhiker's Guide to the Galaxy*, there is a stack of junk mail at the beginning of the game that, if not picked up, precludes the player from winning the game at the end.

In the game Oregon Trail, *if you lose all your oxen, the game becomes UNWINNABLE because you cannot pull your cart.*

vendor trash *(noun)*

Crappy items a player finds in *World of Warcraft* that are only good to sell to vendors.

My character keeps finding wooden armor that is just useless VENDOR TRASH.

video game AI *(noun)*

The computer's control over the nonplayer characters to make them seem more lifelike and also possibly to give them the skills and ability to kick your human ass.

VIDEO GAME AI can compute any math problem but cannot compute the pain within my soul.

Video Game Crash *(proper noun)*

A crash in the video game market in 1983 in North America that sent the industry into a tailspin and many companies into bankruptcy. The success of the NES helped the industry recover.

It's hard to imagine that a VIDEO GAME CRASH could stop the video game industry, which seems unstoppable these days.

virtual economy *(noun)*

An economy that exists in MMORPGs such as *Second Life* and *World of Warcraft* based upon virtual goods that may be exchanged, sometimes using real money. (China has adopted regulations that ban the sale and exchange of virtual items for real money).

A VIRTUAL ECONOMY has all the same problems a regular economy does, including counterfeiting and inflation.

virtual mafia *(noun)*

A situation where veteran players organize themselves and force n00bs to give up game currency for "protection."

The VIRTUAL MAFIA has put me on their hit list. You gotta let me hide in your guild, bro!

visual novel *(noun)*

A genre of video game, popular in Japan, that leads the player through a story with minimal choices and gameplay.

In this short-attention society that is constantly hooked into the Internet, a VISUAL NOVEL is a good compromise between a real novel and watching TV.

GEEK QUIZ

What is the name of the term in video and computer games that describes how the animation displays how a body falls after being killed?

a. Ragdoll physics

b. Insta-corpse

c. Deadman physics

d. Hangman

Answer: a

Vorpal Sword *(proper noun)*

A term used by Lewis Carrol in the poem "Jabberwocky" that has been seen in many RPGs, such as *Baldur's Gate 2* and Dungeons & Dragons.

The VORPAL SWORD was last seen in Tim Burton's Alice in Wonderland.

Walk of Game *(proper noun)*

An area at the Metreon in San Francisco that honors video games and video game characters in the same way the Hollywood Walk of Fame honors movie stars.

Shigeru Miyamoto, who created Mario, The Legend of Zelda, Donkey Kong, *and* Star Fox, *has a lifetime achievement award on the* WALK OF GAME.

wandering monsters *(noun)*

In Dungeon & Dragons, these are the monsters randomly encountered when the player navigates the game environment. They must be defeated to gain experience.

I always thought my father was a Wandering Jew. But when I finally met him, he was more like a WANDERING MONSTER.

Wario *(proper noun)*

A larger, yellower version of Mario who first appeared in 1992 in *Super Mario Land 2* on the Game Boy.

WARIO is like Mario but on steroids.

Wicked Sick *(proper noun)*

Status achieved in the game *Unreal* when a player achieves thirty kills without dying. Comes after Godlike, which is twenty-five kills in a row.

After receiving a WICKED SICK in Torlan during a game of Onslaught, the man was convinced he was a god. In reality, he was just chronically unemployed.

Wii elbow *(noun)*

A painful condition, similar to tennis elbow, that arises from too much use of the Wii.

If you have WII ELBOW, then make sure to get the game Wii Orthopedist.

wood pusher *(noun)*

A very poor chess player, also known as a duffer or patzer.

You no good lousy WOOD PUSHER! You lost in two moves!

woodsball *(noun)*

A paintball game that occurs in a natural environment outdoors.

We were playing WOODSBALL when we were attacked by a bear. Luckily, Jacob and his werewolves showed up to save us.

GEEK QUIZ

For every *Starcraft*, there are dozens of games that never see the light of day. Thousands of titles are produced that fall into obscurity, but not necessarily without good reason. Which of the following is *not* the name of a video game?

a. *Pepsi Man*

b. *Space Bunnies Must Die*

c. *Touch Dic*

d. *Death Soccer: Birmingham*

Answer: d

Zerg rush *(noun)*

A tactic in *Starcraft* where a player sends out attackers immediately. Works best with Zerg.

Me and my wingman ZERG RUSHED a bunch of n00bs, and before they knew what was happening, the game was over.

Zork *(proper noun)*

A 1970s computer game that was one of the first adventure games. Zork is also MIT hacker lingo for a program that is not finished.

The number 69,105 is a running gag in the ZORK games, appearing in many locations. Geek humor, what are you gonna do?

Chapter 8

GEEKOUT AT THE SILVER SCREEN: TELEVISION AND THE MOVIES

Geeks have always been attracted to certain kinds of movies and TV shows, particularly those in the fantasy and science fiction genres such as *Lord of the Rings* and *Star Trek*. Even in the 1960s, old school geeks loved such black-and-white TV shows as *Twilight Zone* and *The Outer Limits*. And when geeks love a movie, they focus on it with much more intensity than the average person. Hence, the Imperial Stormtrooper and Wookie-costumed patrons standing in line for days to be the first to see a *Star Wars* movie.

Today, mainstream movies have gone geek as they increasingly draw their stories from the comic-book world. The San Diego Comic-Con now seems to be more about movies than comic books. This trend will continue in the future in such flourishing franchises as Batman, Iron Man and Spider-man, and as the characters from the Marvel universe assemble in *The Avengers*.

adult puppeteering *(noun)*
Entertainment that uses puppets but deals with adult themes, such as *The Muppet Show* and *Wonder Showzen.*

> *I went to an ADULT PUPPETEERING show in Amsterdam and I haven't been the same since.*

Aint It Cool News *(proper noun)*
A website about comics, movies, and television. Started by Harry Knowles, it has a strong fan base, can influence a film's success (after the site released a negative review of *Batman & Robin*, executives blamed its failure on Internet leaks), and is known for its insider information. The site got its name from a line John Travolta's character speaks in the movie *Broken Arrow:* "Ain't it cool?"

> *The fan comments posted on AINT IT COOL NEWS are always entertaining.*

Alan Smithee *(proper noun)*
A pseudonym used by film directors when they want to disown and take their name off a project. First used in 1969, it has been used dozens of times since.

> *ALAN SMITHEE was used in* Hellraiser: Bloodline. *But it should have also been used in* Look Who's Talking, Look Who's Talking Too, *and* Look Who's Still Talking and Won't Shut Up.

ambiguously gay duo *(noun)*
Derived from the Robert Smigel cartoon of the same name, a term used to describe two guys who are friends but appear to have a relationship that is more than meets the eye.

> *AMBIGUOUSLY GAY DUOS in history include Sacco and Venzetti, Leopold and Loeb, Holmes and Watson, and Batman and Robin.*

Aquafag *(proper noun)*
Used in the show *Entourage* to refer to Vincent Chase's portrayal in the fictional James Cameron movie *Aquaman.*

> *You call me AQUAFAG? The name is Aquaman, and don't forget it. I assure you that the Justice League of America and I will put an end to you.*

GEEK QUIZ

The holodeck has become synonymous with *Star Trek*, but it was not always around. The holodeck made its first appearance in which incarnation of *Star Trek*?

a. *Star Trek: The Animated Series*

b. *Star Trek: The Original Series*

c. *Star Trek: The Next Generation*

d. *Star Trek: The Motion Picture*

Answer: a

Ash *(proper noun)*

Main character and demon ass-kicker of the *Evil Dead* series, played by Bruce "the Chin" Campbell. His catchphrases include "Who wants some?" and "Hail to the king, baby."

When are they going to be bring ASH back for a new Evil Dead *movie?*

AT-AT *(proper noun)*

Short for All Terrain Armored Transport. An Imperial walker first seen in the battle of Hoth in *The Empire Strikes Back*. The AT-AT resembles a four-legged animal, and the designers modeled its walking style after that of elephants. The two-legged version is referred to as an AT-ST, or All Terrain Scout Transport.

An AT-AT and a mûmak enter the Thunderdome. Two will enter, one will leave.

AURYN *(proper noun)*

A talisman with magical powers given to Atreyu in *The Neverending Story,* it assists him in his quest to find the Childlike Empress.

In a battle between Atreyu and Frodo, who would win? The AURYN would probably be the One Ring's bitch.

GEEK QUIZ

From the cantina scene to Jabba the Hutt's palace, *Star Wars* is known for having scenes with a diverse crowd of aliens, and they all have names. Which is *not* the name of a *Star Wars* alien that has appeared in the movies?

a. Gamorrean

b. Kitonak

c. Utai

d. Rylan

Answer: d

---

avatard *(noun)*
A fan of the TV show *Avatar: The Last Airbender.*
> *AVATARDS were reportedly very disappointed by* The Last Airbender *movie.*

away team *(noun)*
A term first used on *Star Trek: The Next Generation* for a starship team that beams down to the surface of a planet, usually to investigate strange phenomena.
> *Why do the most senior crewmembers always go on the AWAY TEAM? Why not send in a few red shirts?*

Bad Robot *(proper noun)*
The production company founded by J. J. Abrams. Bad Robot has produced many geek favorites, including the TV shows *Alias, Lost, Fringe,* and the 2009 *Star Trek* film.
> *BAD ROBOT!*

bah weep granah weep ninni bong *(phrase)*
The universal greeting in the original cartoon *Transformers* movie. Used by the Autobots to befriend the Junkticons.
> *How do you get a one-armed Autobot out of a tree? Say, "BAH WEEP GRANAH WEEP NINNI BONG" and wave at him. Just kidding, some of my best friends are Autobots.*

Batman: The Animated Series *(proper noun)*
A cartoon that ran from 1992 to 1995, chronicling the adventures of the DC Comics superhero Batman. Considered one of the best cartoons ever made, the series was much more adult-oriented than most cartoons of the time, notable not only for its dark animated style but for being one of the first cartoons to portray real firearms (most cartoons at the time used laser weapons of some sort to heighten the unreality). To this day, it is still considered one of the definitive incarnations of Batman. Mark "Skywalker" Hamill voiced the Joker.

> BATMAN: THE ANIMATED SERIES *may be the best TV cartoon ever.*

bat phone *(noun)*
A red-colored phone used by Commissioner Gordon to call Batman in the 1960s *Batman* TV show.

> BAT PHONE *can be used as a term for a private telephone call that is of high importance.*

Battle Royale Act *(proper noun)*
As seen in the film *Battle Royale*, based on a novel by Koushun Takami. In a fascist version of Japan, the authorities take one high school class each year and give them weapons. Then the students are forced to fight each other until only one student survives.

> *Fed up with his kids, the teacher came up with a new game for the kids to play, and the BATTLE ROYALE ACT was on.*

Bender *(proper noun)*
The wise-cracking immoral robot in the TV series *Futurama*.

> BENDER *to his friends, his full name is Bender Bending Rodriguez.*

benders *(noun)*
A term used in *Avatar: The Last Airbender* for people (and sometimes even animals) that have the ability to manipulate one of the four elements: water, earth, air, and fire. Only the Avatar can master all four elements.

> *I wonder if there is a BENDER for the element of "heart," like in* Captain Planet.

GEEK QUIZ

Futurama is a show every geek should watch. From the jokes about science to the satire of modern technology, it is always on the money. What is *not* the name of a fictional TV show on the animated show *Futurama*?

a. *Everybody Loves Hypnotoad*

b. *All My Circuits*

c. *Little House on Uranus*

d. *Entertainment and Alien Invasion Tonight*

Answer: c

Boba Fett *(proper noun)*
A popular hero in the *Star Wars* universe who wears Mandalorian armor and works as a bounty hunter. The character first appeared onscreen in the 1978 *Star Wars Christmas Special*.

BOBA FETT is so popular that everyone knows about him. But did you know his helmet contains a retractable straw? No? Ha!

GEEK FACT

The first Boba Fett action figure advertised by Kenner could only be purchased through the mail and was advertised as having a backpack that fired a mini rocket. But due to safety concerns, later figures were released with the rocket permanently attached. The few figures released with the rocket-firing backpack have since become valued collector's items, selling for well over $10,000.

Bodhi *(proper noun)*
Also known as Bodhisatva, the surfing leader of the bank robbing Ex-presidents and spiritual guru in the film *Point Break*, opposite FBI Agent, Keanu "whoa" Reeves.

I wish I could play BODHI in Point Break Live!, *the live theatre version of* Point Break.

Bog of Eternal Stench *(proper noun)*
As seen in the Jim Henson film *Labyrinth*, it is a gurgling and burping swamp that will make you smell bad forever even if you only put one toe in it.
I switched my ex-girlfriend's body lotion with samples from the BOG OF ETERNAL STENCH.

Bossk *(proper noun)*
The Trandoshan bounty hunter in one scene of *The Empire Strikes Back* (the one that looks like a bipedal reptilian swine with a bad attitude). The other bounty hunters in the scene were Boba Fett, Dengar, Zuckuss, IG-88, and 4-LOM. Bossk was also seen in Jabba's sail barge in *Return of the Jedi*.
My date last night looked like BOSSK'S twin sister.

Brannigan's Law *(proper noun)*
On the TV show *Futurama,* a parody of *Star Trek's* "Prime Directive." Named for Captain Zapp Brannigan, it states that one cannot interfere with an undeveloped planet. However, Brannigan himself admits that even he doesn't understand it.
"BRANNIGAN'S LAW is like Brannigan's love: hard and fast." — Captain Zapp Brannigan

Broken Lizard *(proper noun)*
The comedy troupe responsible for hilarious films like *Super Troopers* and *Beerfest*.
BROKEN LIZARD's most recent project is the movie The Slammin' Salmon.

Bruce Timm *(proper noun)*
An American animator and comic book artist, most notable for being one of the primary creators of *Batman: The Animated Series,* as well as other DC Animated Universe shows like *Superman: The Animated Series, Batman Beyond,* and *Justice League.*
BRUCE TIMM'S style of animation was influenced by the 1950s and 1960s art deco style.

Buffy the Vampire Slayer *(proper noun)*
A character first seen in the 1982 film of the same name, Buffy achieved true fame in the ensuing TV series, which ran from 1997 to 2003. The show spawned the spinoff *Angel,* and even after the show's cancellation, the story continued as a comic book series.
The TV series was cool, but the best part of the BUFFY THE VAMPIRE SLAYER *movie was Pee-wee Herman as a vampire.*

bullet time *(noun)*
A special effect, as seen in *The Matrix* series where time slows down or stops with the characters in dramatic or acrobatic positions.
When my comic collection began falling off the shelf, everything began moving in BULLET TIME.

bumps *(noun)*
Short fifteen-second breaks placed between commercials to state the title of a program and the name of the network.
I am so disappointed when a BUMP ends because I want my show to begin!

GEEK QUIZ

The TV show *The Big Bang Theory* really gives some insight into the geek world. The two characters on *The Big Bang Theory*, Leonard Hofstadter and Sheldon Cooper, both work at:

a. Caltech

b. MIT

c. UC Berkeley

d. Harvard

Answer: a

Centauri *(proper noun)*
In *The Last Starfighter* movie, he was the inventor of the game *Starfighter* who recruited Alex Rogan to become a real starfighter to aid the Rylan Star League in its fight against the Ko-Dan armada.
CENTAURI's car/starship and other effects in the movie were the earliest examples of CGI. And it shows.

CGI *(noun)*
Short for computer-generated imagery. Special effects created by a computer used in movies and television using programs like Maya.
 CGI is responsible for revolutionizing the way movies are made—a curse and a blessing, because so many movies emphasize CGI over storytelling.

Chekhov's gun *(noun)*
A technique commonly used in film and literature where an item that is introduced casually at the beginning of a story ends up playing a major role later on.
 The first golden snitch that Harry Potter catches is a CHEKHOV'S GUN, because he opens it in The Deathly Hallows *to reveal the Resurrection Stone.*

Chewie *(phrase)*
The geek equivalent of calling out "Shotgun!" Because Chewbacca (Chewie) was Han Solo's faithful copilot in the *Star Wars* movies and always sat to Han's right, when three or more people are headed for the car, the geek who wants to ride in the front seat must call out, "Chewie!"
 CHEWIE!

chick flick *(noun)*
A movie—usually a story dealing with romance, relationships, or horses—that appeals to a wide female audience. Men will watch chick flicks but generally do so only in the hopes of being suitably rewarded afterward.
 Don't know what a CHICK FLICK is? Go rent Under the Tuscan Sun, Dirty Dancing, Steel Magnolias, *or* The Horse Whisperer.

chick fu *(noun)*
Any movie or TV show that involves two or more women engaged in a martial arts fight—preferably while dressed in black leather.
 Great examples of CHICK FU in recent years include the TV show Alias, *the so-so movie* Underworld, *and Ang Lee's* Crouching Tiger, Hidden Dragon.

chicken walker *(noun)*

A type of mecha that has rear-facing knee joints and walks like a bird. Examples are Ed-209 and the AT-ST of Star Wars.

If you ever face a CHICKEN WALKER, remember that its weakness is being tripped, because it will not be able to get back up.

Colbert Report *(proper noun)*

A news show on Comedy Central starring Stephen Colbert as a parody of Bill O'Reilly.

Not many people realize that Stephen Colbert is actually much different, nicer, and quieter in reality than he is on the COLBERT REPORT.

cyberbrain sclerosis *(noun)*

A fictional disease that infects a person's cyberbrain implant in *The Ghost in the Shell* series and causes memory loss and difficulty in speaking.

HAL may have suffered from an undiagnosed case of CYBERBRAIN SCLEROSIS.

dark deco *(noun)*

The design style of *Batman: The Animated Series*—so called by the producers because of its art deco style combined with gothic imagery.

I am redesigning my cubicle to be DARK DECO to show the office that I am a tortured soul.

GEEK FACT

Etymology: "Batman" comes from the English word "bat," meaning well, a bat, and the English word "man," meaning, you know, "guy."

Dark Passenger *(proper noun)*

The subconscious voice of Dexter Morgan that drives him to kill criminals in the HBO series *Dexter*. The Dark Defender is a comic book character based on Dexter and the Dark Passenger.

"I certainly don't talk about it. But it's there. Always. This DARK PASSENGER." —Dexter

Dark Side *(proper noun)*
In *Star Wars,* the negative side of the Force, giving power through aggression, haste, and emotions like fear, anger, and hate. Darth Vader and Emperor Palpatine are both masters of the Dark Side and use it to control the Empire.

"If you only knew the power of the DARK SIDE!" —Darth Vader

8

GEEK QUIZ

Match the dark side with the country responsible:

1. Germany	a. Making us watch those "Ricola" commercials over and over again
2. Japan	b. Holocaust, invention of industrial music
3. Switzerland	c. Every bad foreign policy decision 1945–present
4. United States	d. Bataan Death March

Answer: 1. b 2. d 3. a 4. c

Darth Maul *(proper noun)*
The apprentice of Darth Sidious in *Star Wars Episode I: The Phantom Menace.* Darth Maul wields a dual-edged lightsaber and kills Qui-Gon Jinn before being split in half by Obi-wan Kenobi.

DARTH MAUL was one of the coolest Star Wars *characters. Too bad he dies so fast.*

GEEK FACT

Darth Maul was played by actor and martial artist extraordinaire Ray Park, who would later go on to work in such films as Tim Burton's *Sleepy Hollow,* Bryan Singer's *X-Men,* and the NBC hit series *Heroes.*

Darth Vader *(proper noun)*
Also known as the "Dark Lord of the Sith," Darth Vader is the enemy of the Jedi, and master of the Dark Side. He wears cybernetic armor that keeps him alive and gives him a powerful deep voice that erases from our memory the whiny brat from the prequels.

DARTH VADER's armor was influenced by the samurai helmet and the villain The Lightning, from the TV series, The Fighting Devil Dogs.

GEEK FACT

Geeks can wait in line for days. Even *Twilight* draws lines that last forever. When the *Star Wars* prequels came out, fans were known to start waiting in line six to seven weeks before the opening. When *Revenge of the Sith* was released, fans started lining up forty-six days before opening night at the Grauman's Chinese Theater. Unfortunately for them, it was the wrong theatre.

Death Star *(proper noun)*
In the *Star Wars* universe, a giant space station shaped like a planet that is the ultimate weapon and can destroy a planet with a single blast.

In Kevin Smith's movie Clerks, *a character sympathizes with the innocent contract workers on the DEATH STAR when it was destroyed.*

development hell *(noun)*
When a movie has been optioned for development but for some reason just can't get past preproduction.

Movies that should have stayed in DEVELOPMENT HELL include The Bucket List *and* The Notebook.

GEEK QUIZ

Did you know that Sean Connery turned down the role of Gandalf in *The Lord of the Rings* films? But he is not the first actor to turn down famous roles. Steve McQueen is famous for doing just that. Which of the following films did Steve McQueen *not* turn down for the starring role?

a. *Breakfast at Tiffany's*

b. *Dirty Harry*

c. *Apocalypse Now*

d. *The Sting*

Answer: d

deus ex machina *(noun)*

A plot device where a seemingly unsolvable problem is solved by an improbable last-second solution or act of god. The term is Latin and literally means "god from the machine." It originates from Greek tragedy where a crane (the machine) would lower an actor (playing a god) into the scene.

A DEUS EX MACHINA is like a plant, you can't wait for it to appear or it will never come.

GEEK FACT

Connery turned down the role of Gandalf in Peter Jackson's *The Lord of the Rings* films because he did not understand the script. When the films became smash hits worldwide, lauded by both audiences and critics alike, Connery regretted his decision—so much so that he accepted the role of Allan Quartermain in the movie version of *The League of Extraordinary Gentlemen*—even though he admitted he didn't understand this one either. *League* was panned by most critics, hated by most fans of the comic book, and did only modest business at the box office. Sean Connery announced his retirement shortly thereafter, saying it was due mostly to the "idiots now in Hollywood."

Dimension X *(noun)*

Another dimension in *Teenage Mutant Ninja Turtles*, home to Krang and the technodrome.

It is still unclear whether DIMENSION X is actually another dimension or just further out into outer space.

Doctor Who *(proper noun)*

The long-running BBC television show about the alien humanoid doctor who travels in the TARDIS through time and space. The doctor is also a Time Lord, and therefore can create a new body, which explains why there have been so many different actors playing the role throughout the run of the show. From 1967 to 1978, more than 100 *Doctor Who* episodes were wiped over by the BBC to make room for new material, with no other copies in existence.

"I'll watch the last 24 minutes of DOCTOR WHO, although at this point it's more like Doctor Why Bother." —Sheldon on *The Big Bang Theory*

DreamWorks face *(noun)*

The face that all the main characaters in a DreamWorks computer-animated movie make, as seen on a multitude of movie posters, where one eyebrow is lowered in an exaggerated fashion and a sly smile is given.

After I let out a fart in class, I gave the DREAMWORKS FACE.

Easter egg *(noun)*

A hidden message or joke left by the creator of a software program, game, movie, or DVD. Famous Easter eggs include Hitchcock appearing in his own films, or R2-D2 floating in space in the 2009 *Star Trek* film.

Surprisingly, there were no EASTER EGGS in Mel Gibson's The Passion of the Christ.

GEEK FACT

Apple computers had a problem early on with a company called Franklin Computers cloning their Apple II computer, but eventually won in a lawsuit. After that, Apple placed an 'easter egg' in the ROM in the form of a picture of a man behind bars with the message "Stolen from Apple," which would appear if certain keys were pressed to prove the product was from Apple.

GEEKTIONARY

ED-209 *(proper noun)*
The heavily armed police bipedal robot that Robocop replaced after a malfunction resulting in the death of an OCP executive. Phil Tippett, who worked on the special effects of ED-209, was also a supervisor of special effects in the movies *The Empire Strikes Back, Robocop,* and *Jurassic Park.*

ED-209, when turned over and unable to get up, acts and sounds like a little harmless baby.

GEEK QUIZ

What is the name of the actor who played Gilligan, the goofy red-shirt wearing first mate of the SS *Minnow*, in the 1960s TV show *Gilligan's Island*?

a. Alan Hale, Jr.

b. Jim Backus

c. Bob Denver

d. Sherwood Schwartz

Answer: c

Falkor *(proper noun)*
A giant luck dragon that looks like a dog but is actually very friendly and will fly you anywhere you want to go, as seen in *The Neverending Story.*

I had a dream I was flying on FALKOR while music by Enigma was playing and we were on our way to Candy Land.

fanwanking *(noun)*
1.The attempts of fans of anime to try to fill plot holes in a work. These attempts are not canon. 2. The inclusion in a movie or TV show of what the fans desire just to make them happy.

Including Boba Fett in the prequels is an obvious case of FAN-WANKING because he is so popular among Star Wars *fans.*

Firefly *(proper noun)*

A science-fiction television show created by Joss Whedon, it was noted for being a mix of the science fiction and Western genres. Despite being much beloved by fans, critics' reactions were mixed, and the show failed to find a wide audience and only lasted one season before being cancelled. Fans of the show refer to themselves as "Browncoats," after the Western-style duster worn by the show's main character.

After FIREFLY *was cancelled, Whedon took the story to the movies with the film* Serenity. *The movie was generally well received by critics but had a disappointing box office run.*

five-point palm exploding heart technique *(noun)*

A type of death touch portrayed in the movie *Kill Bill* where the attacker touches certain pressure points, causing death after the victim takes five steps.

The Bride: *"What, pray tell, is a FIVE-POINT PALM EXPLODING HEART TECHNIQUE?"*

Bill: *"Quite simply, the deadliest blow in all of the martial arts. He hits you with his fingertips, at five different pressure points on your body. And then he lets you walk away. But once you've taken five steps, your heart explodes inside your body, and you fall to the floor dead."*

Fizzbin *(proper noun)*

A card game created by Captain Kirk in the original *Star Trek* series with an intentionally complicated rule set used to distract his captor, so that he can escape.

The first rule of FIZZBIN is: You don't talk about FIZZBIN.

GEEK FACT

What are some imaginary games played in sci-fi? There is Tri-Dimensional Chess in *Star Trek*, Dejarik (holographic chess) in *Star Wars*, Stealth Chess in *Discworld*, Pai-Sho in *Avatar: The Last Airbender*, and Sabacc, the card game Han Solo was playing when he won the Millennium Falcon,

---

flux capacitor *(noun)*
In the *Back to the Future* films, a device used in Doc Brown's time machine that is shaped as an upside down *Y* with three flashing lights. It is what makes time travel possible.

I don't care if it has a FLUX CAPACITOR. I want to see the Carfax.

Forbidden Planet *(proper noun)*
A 1956 movie, considered to be one of the greatest science-fiction films ever made. It is essentially a re-imagining of Shakespeare's *The Tempest*. The movie had a huge influence upon the genre and was one of the primary inspirations for Gene Roddenberry in creating *Star Trek*.

FORBIDDEN PLANET . . . Greatest. Movie. Ever.

The Force *(proper noun)*
In the *Star Wars* universe, a mystical "force" that gives the Jedi their power. The Force has both a light and a dark side.

"The Force is what gives a Jedi his power. It's an energy field created by all living things. It surrounds us and penetrates us. It binds the galaxy together." —Obi-Wan "Old Ben" Kenobi

frak *(noun)*
A term used on the television show *Battlestar Galactica* to censor the word that begins with an F and ends in U-C-K. And no, it's not "firetruck."

Holy FRAK! A group of Cylons want to settle this dispute in a street-level dance off!

Frat Pack *(proper noun)*
The group of comedians often seen in the same movies together, including Vince Vaughn, Ben Stiller, Owen Wilson, and Will Ferrell.

Other famous "Packs" other than the FRAT PACK are the Rat Pack, the Brat Pack, and the Putz Pack (Justin Bieber, Ashton Kutcher, Clay Aiken).

Freaks and Geeks *(proper noun)*
An hour-long TV show about high school students in the early 1980s. It was produced by Judd Apatow and ran for a year starting in 1999. Despite being critically acclaimed (it still makes critics' lists of one of the best TV shows of all time), the show never fared well in the ratings and only lasted one season. It has since gained a cult following.

FREAKS AND GEEKS starred Apatow regulars Seth Rogen, Jason Segel, and James Franco—all of whom lead better lives than you.

frill *(phrase)*

In the Sci-Fi Channel (now Syfy) series *Farscape*, the substituted word for the word that begins with an F and ends in U-C-K. And we're still not talking about "firetruck."

FRILL you, stupid frakker.

Fritz the Cat *(proper noun)*

The most famous comic strip of Robert Crumb, about a cat and his adventures, many which are sexual in nature. Adapted into a hit film in 1972 by Ralph Bakshi. The film earned an X-rating.

FRITZ THE CAT, and especially later strips by Robert Crumb, were aided by his use of LSD.

Futurama *(proper noun)*

A science-fiction TV sitcom created by Matt Groening (one of the creators of *The Simpsons*). The show lasted four seasons on the Fox network before being cancelled, but thanks to the show's huge following made a comeback on DVD. New episodes premiered on Comedy Central in 2010.

The main character on FUTURAMA is Philip J. Fry, a pizza delivery guy who inadvertently locked himself in a cryogenic booth in the year 2000 and woke up in the year 2999.

Game of Death *(proper noun)*

Bruce Lee's final film, left unfinished, where Bruce would have to make his way to the top of a pagoda, fighting martial arts experts like Kareem Abdul-Jabbar on the way.

The tracksuit worn in GAME OF DEATH, which was yellow and black, inspired Uma Thurman's fashion in Tarantino's Kill Bill.

Gene Roddenbery *(proper noun)*

Eugene Wesley "Gene" Roddenberry was an American screenwriter and producer, most famous for creating *Star Trek*.

After his death, GENE RODDENBERRY'S ashes were launched into space aboard a Pegasus XL rocket. Other remains onboard included the ashes of Timothy Leary.

General Grievous *(proper noun)*
The cyborg general in command of the Separatists in *Star Wars Episode III: The Revenge of the Sith*. Grievous has four arms that each wield the lightsaber of a Jedi he has killed.
> *GENERAL GRIEVOUS was created by George Lucas to foreshadow Darth Vader, by creating a cyborg character.*

Genesis Device *(proper noun)*
Introduced in *Star Trek II: The Wrath of Khan*, the device had the ability to "create life from lifelessness." Although intended for good, the film's villain seeks to use it for his own nefarious schemes.
> *Terraforming is a staple of many science-fiction stories, but what those stories did over decades, the GENESIS DEVICE did in minutes.*

George Pal *(proper noun)*
Born György Pál Marczincsak, George Pal was a Hungarian-American filmmaker responsible for some of the most beloved science-fiction films of all time, especially the 1953 version of *The War of the Worlds* and the 1960 version of *The Time Machine* (both based upon stories by H. G. Wells).
> *Although he is best remembered for the live-action films he produced, GEORGE PAL began his career as an animator.*

Glasgow smile *(noun)*
A facial cut caused by slicing each sides of someone's mouth, as seen by the torture-loving character Kakihara in the manga and live action movie *Ichi the Killer*. Also seen in the Joker as played by Heath Ledger.
> *Do you know where I got this GLASGOW SMILE? Why so serious?*

go motion *(noun)*
A type of stop-motion animation developed by Industrial Light and Magic for the *Star Wars* movies, where instead of having a model remain still in a stop-motion frame, the model will be moving slightly to give a more fluid effect.
> *GO MOTION was going to be used for* Jurassic Park *before Steven Spielberg decided to use CGI.*

Gobots *(proper noun)*

A toy line and cartoon in the '80s that was a competitor with the Transformers. Included robots such as Cy-Kill, Cop-Tur, and Leader-1.

It was always awkward trying to integrate GOBOTS and Transformers toys together into a play session. It always seemed a little wrong.

grindhouse *(noun)*

A movie theatre that shows low-budget exploitation cinema. The films often contain sex, violence, and bizarre plots.

We the authors are too young to have appreciated porno theaters and GRINDHOUSES, but I have been to a few and let me tell you, losing them was a real loss to American culture.

guerrilla filmmaking *(noun)*

A type of filmmaking shot on a very low budget using friends of the filmmaker and whatever props were on hand.

El Mariachi and Pi were both made using GUERRILLA FILMMAKING.

gun fu *(noun)*

The use of a gun in a special way, derived from martial arts, as seen in many John Woo films, where the characters wield a gun in each hand, or in *Equilibrium* where it is called "gun kata."

The most advanced technique in GUN FU involves holding the pistol sideways like a gangsta.

Hab sosli quch *(phrase)*

Klingon for "Your mother has a smooth forehead!" The worst possible insult.

You dare to cut off my Klingon Bird of Prey without signaling? HAB SOSLI QUCH!

GEEK FACT

More Klingon "Yo mama" jokes:

- Yo mama's so ugly, it would take 100 light-years for her to couple with a Gorn.
- Yo mama's so nasty she brings her own crabs to the Crab Nebula.
- Yo mama's so hairless you can see what's on her mind.

hack the Gibson *(verb)*
To break into a computer from a remote location and steal information. Used in the movie *Hackers*, the Gibson is a supercomputer named after William Gibson, author of *Neuromancer*.
I tried to HACK THE GIBSON and got arrested, but Angelina Jolie didn't come to save me like she did in the movie.

HAL 9000 *(proper noun)*
Short for Heuristically programmed ALgorithmic Computer. An artificial computer that serves as an antagonist in *2001: A Space Odyssey*. HAL manages to kill all but one of the crew before being deactivated by the one survivor.
The name HAL is thought to come from IBM because the position in the alphabet of the letters I-B-M each occur exactly one letter after the letters H-A-L.

Hamsterdam *(proper noun)*
On the HBO series *The Wire*, the urban area where drugs were legalized under a renegade police major.
The cops don't bother us at all even though they know we party. It's like our own personal HAMSTERDAM.

Harley Quinn *(proper noun)*
A villain created by Paul Dini and Bruce Timm for *Batman: The Animated Series*. Dr. Harleen Frances Quinzel was a psychologist who fell in love with the Joker and joined him in a life of crime, taking the name "Harley Quinn," which is a play on the word "harlequin." The character proved to be so popular that she was adopted into comic books, video games, and the *Birds of Prey* TV show, and has been rumored to be featured in upcoming Batman films.
Want to attract the romantic attention of your favorite geek? Show up at his house in a HARLEY QUINN costume.

GEEK FACT
How popular is Harley Quinn among geeks? Famed geek filmmaker Kevin Smith named his daughter Harley Quinn.

Hawk the Slayer *(proper noun)*

A 1980 sword & sorcery film. It was almost universally panned by critics but gained a huge cult following after multiple late-night viewings on Showtime. The film was noted for its Morricone-inspired discoesque soundtrack. Along with John Milius's *Conan the Barbarian* film, *Hawk the Slayer* probably inspired more D&D campaigns in the '80s than any other movie. Rumors of a sequel, *Hawk the Hunter*, have sprouted in recent years, but nothing has come to fruition so far.

> *I probably watched* HAWK THE SLAYER *at least fifty times when I was a kid. Favorite character? Crow the elf. Orlando Bloom's Legolas had nothin' on Crow!*

GEEK FACT

John Terry, the actor who played Hawk the Slayer, rose to geek fame again on the TV series *Lost*, where he played Jack Sheppard's father.

Heisenberg *(proper noun)*

Famous physicist responsible for the Heisenberg uncertainty principle, also the black-hat-wearing alter ego of scientist and drug kingpin Walter White on *Breaking Bad*. The Heisenberg uncertainty principle, posited by Werner Heisenberg in 1927, states that it is impossible to determine both the position and velocity of a quantum object such as an electron with any certainty. This principle is not based upon a lack in measuring capability, but instead refers to the fundamental nature of quantum mechanics

> *I would explain to you what the* HEISENBERG *uncertainty principle is in detail, but the truth is I'm not really certain.*

holodeck *(noun)*

A room in a *Star Trek* starship that simulates reality according to the user's desires.

> *The* HOLODECK *is the ultimate virtual reality fantasy.*

GEEK FACT

The transporters in *Star Trek: The Next Generation* are able to overcome the issues that exist as a result of the Heisenberg uncertainty principle by the use of "Heisenberg compensators." In 1994, when *Star Trek* technical advisor, Michael Okuda, was asked by *Time* magazine "How do the Heisenberg Compensators work?" he responded "It works very well, thank you." This illustrates a typical device used in hard science fiction, where such impossibilities as faster-than-light travel are acknowledged but vaguely explained away.

hoverboard *(noun)*
In the movies *Back to the Future II* and *III*, the hoverboard was the successor to the skateboard, and it used hover technology rather than wheels.
Every time I'm in traffic in Los Angeles, I wish I had my HOVERBOARD.

GEEK FACT

Being civilized Starfleet officers, the crew of the *Enterprise* most often used the holodeck to play detective. However, the geekiest geek on the *Enterprise*, Lieutenant Reginald Barkley, is the only one to use the holodeck to pick up women. Imaginary women, true, but you gotta hand it to the geek for having his priorities straight. The character of Lieutenant Barkley was played by Dwight Schultz, who also played the geekiest geek on the TV series *The A-Team*.

Imaginationland *(proper noun)*
In *South Park*, a land where everything that imagination has created lives. Some residents are Count Chocula, John Wayne's character from *True Grit*, and Dick Tracy.
Who would you like to meet in IMAGINATIONLAND? All of the Disney princesses.

inverse ninja law *(phrase)*

The law that states that ninjas in larger groups are weaker, as seen in many movies where ninjas attack the hero one at a time, and are always easily dispatched, whereas a single ninja is much harder to defeat.

> *Back off, there is only one ninja here. Don't you know the INVERSE NINJA LAW? He must be a worthy foe if he is by himself.*

J. J. Abrams *(proper noun)*

Writer, director, producer, and composer. He either created or helped to create such geek favorites as the TV shows *Alias*, *Lost*, and *Fringe*. Abrams directed the 2009 reboot *Star Trek* film.

> *J. J. ABRAMS also wrote the 1998 film* Armageddon. *Nobody's perfect.*

J. Michael Straczynski *(proper noun)*

Fondly known as JMS in geekdom. A prolific writer of many geek favorites. He created the TV series *Babylon 5* and *Jeremiah*, wrote the screenplay for the Clint Eastwood film *Changeling*, and has written acclaimed comic books for Marvel, DC, and other publishers. He was also commissioned to write the screenplay for a Silver Surfer movie, which even he admits will probably never be made, and a remake of the classic *Forbidden Planet*.

> *J. MICHAEL STRACZYNSKI supposedly wrote the script for* Ninja Assassin *in only fifty-three hours. Considering it was a Wachowski movie, that was probably fifty-one hours too long.*

Jedi *(proper noun)*

The mystic warriors of the *Star Wars* films who use the Force and wield lightsabers.

> *"I was once a JEDI knight, the same as your father." —Obi-Wan "Old Ben" Kenobi*

GEEK FACT

The origin of the word "Jedi" is from the Japanese *jidai geki*, which basically means a period adventure drama. Japanese cinema, especially the films of Akira Kurosawa, were a huge influence on George Lucas in the creation of *Star Wars*. Interestingly, Akira Kurosawa was strongly influenced by western filmmaker John Ford.

Jedi mind trick *(noun)*
A tactic used by a Jedi to make a weak-minded individual obey a Jedi's wishes.

I used a JEDI MIND TRICK to make a chick hook up with me in five minutes.

Joss Whedon *(proper noun)*
Writer and director of such geek favorites as *Buffy the Vampire Slayer*, *Angel*, *Firefly*, *Serenity*, and several comic book series. He is slotted to direct the *Avengers* movie.

JOSS WHEDON fans can be a bit intense.

kaiju *(noun)*
Translated from Japanese, it means "strange beast." They are seen as giant monsters that terrorize cities in Tokusatsu films, which are live-action sci-fi or fantasy Japanese films. Mothra and Godzilla are kaiju.

Godzilla is the most famous KAIJU.

Kessel run *(noun)*
In the *Star Wars* universe, a smugglers' route used to move glitterstim spice out of Kessel, made difficult because one needs to evade detection by Imperial starships.

Han Solo made the KESSEL RUN in less than twelve parsecs (a unit of distance) by taking a short cut past the Maw black hole cluster.

key grip *(noun)*
In filmmaking, a person who works on lights, the movement of the camera, and placing the camera in its appropriate place on dollys and cranes. They help in safety monitoring, construction, and other administrative duties.

No one has figured out what a KEY GRIP does until now. Finally, the mystery is solved! Now onto what the Best Boy does.

Khan *(proper noun)*
Khan Noonien Singh, a genetically altered human being and Captain Kirk's greatest enemy. First introduced in the original *Star Trek* episode "Space Seed," he returned in glory in *Star Trek II: Wrath of Khan.* Played by Ricardo Montalban, Khan is considered to be one of the best onscreen villains of all time.

"KHAAAAAAAAAAAAANNN!"

GEEK FACT

According to Nicholas Meyer, the director of *Star Trek II: The Wrath of Khan*, those were indeed Ricardo Montalban's real pecs.

Kobayashi Maru *(proper noun)*
A test in the *Star Trek* universe given to cadets in Starfleet Academy to determine their character strength in a no-win situation. Captain Kirk is the only cadet to have ever passed the test, which he did by cheating.

My girlfriend wants me to watch either Steel Magnolias *or* Beaches. *It's a lose-lose KOBAYASHI MARU situation.*

lanista *(noun)*
A manager of gladiators as represented in the movie *Spartacus* and Starz series *Spartacus: Blood and Sand* by the character Batiatus.

I am not surprised the gladiators revolted with Spartacus, considering the way their LANISTA treated them.

GEEK QUIZ

What 1960s television science-fiction series opened with strange visuals of an oscilloscope display?

a. *The Outer Limits*

b. *Science Fiction Theatre*

c. *Dark Shadows*

d. *The Twilight Zone*

Answer: a

---

late-night wars *(noun)*
The backstage political maneuvering that occurs with late-night talk show hosts, as seen when Johnny Carson retired and Jay Leno and David Letterman were both up for the spot.

The LATE-NIGHT WARS were in the news recently when Jay Leno came and took over for the funnier Conan O'Brien.

Lebowski Fest *(noun)*

An annual gathering to celebrate the movie *The Big Lebowski*. People dress as characters from the movie, drink White Russians, and participate in various games and events.

The LEBOWSKI FEST shows us that there is a Dude in all of us.

ludicrous speed *(noun)*

From the Mel Brooks' film *Space Balls*, it is a parody of science-fiction tropes like "light speed" or "hyperspace" (from *Star Wars*) and "warp speed" (from *Star Trek*). When light speed is too slow, ludicrous speed is the fastest speed possible, and results in everything going plaid.

Colonel Sandurz: "Prepare the ship for light speed."
Dark Helmet: "No, no, no. Light speed is too slow."
Colonel Sandurz: "Light speed too slow?"
Dark Helmet: "Yes. We're gonna have to go right to LUDICROUS SPEED."

Luxo Jr. *(proper noun)*

An award-winning computer animated short by Pixar featuring a desk lamp character.

The LUXO JR. lamp is seen in the Pixar title card that opens each Pixar film.

Lycan *(noun)*

Werewolves in the *Underworld* movies that are immortal and whose bite spreads the Lycan virus, which causes the bitten to become a Lycan. Lycans are different than werewolves in that they have a greater ability to control their transformation from human to wolf and back again. The first Lycan was played by Michael Sheen, who also played David Frost in *Frost/Nixon*. "Lycan" is derived from *lykos,* the Greek word for "wolf."

If all LYCANS looked like Kate Beckinsale, they'd be much more popular.

Lynchian *(adjective)*

A movie or scene that is strange, weird, and shows the underlying macabre nature of the ordinary world, much like a David Lynch film.

The most LYNCHIAN recurring shot is a close-up of a cigarette as it burns, a metaphor for something really profound or something— like a burning cigarette.

MacGuffin *(noun)*
Sometimes spelled "Maguffin," it is a plot device used to advance a story, popularized by Alfred Hitchcock. It is the center of the plot and what is being pursued by the protagonist.

Famous MACGUFFINS are the Holy Grail in Indiana Jones and the Last Crusade, *the glowing contents of the briefcase in* Pulp Fiction, *and the continuum transfunctioner in* Dude, Where's My Car? *All three great movies btw.*

MacGyver *(noun)*
Word for a person who has a talent for taking mundane objects and making them useful, as seen on the television show *MacGyver*, where MacGyver could escape any situation using everyday objects such as an empty bottle and a paper clip.

My little brother is a real MACGYVER, the little @#$%!!!.

Madmartigan *(proper noun)*
The greatest swordsman that ever lived, played by Val Kilmer in the movie *Willow*, opposite Warwick Davis, who played the Ewok Wicket in the *Return of the Jedi*.

Val Kilmer's portrayal of MADMARTIGAN falls into what film critics call Kilmer's "pre-fat-disgusting-pig" years as an actor.

Manson lamps *(phrase)*
In *The Sopranos*, it is the term Tony Soprano uses to describe Richie Aprile's glare—a reference to infamous cult leader and murderer Charles Manson. Can be used to describe any crazed, maniacal glare.

"Quit givin' me those Manson lamps." —Tony Soprano

Masturbating Bear *(proper noun)*
A character on the *Late Night with Conan O'Brien*. A bear wearing a diaper that masturbates.
Honey, where did you put my MASTURBATING BEAR?

Matrixism *(proper noun)*
A religion based on movie *The Matrix.*
Census time! For "Religion," should I claim MATRIXISM or Jediism?

Matrix of Leadership *(proper noun)*
A powerful talisman that is given to the leader of the Autobots, who receives the title Prime.
Whenever the MATRIX OF LEADERSHIP is opened, '80s heavy metal music begins to play.

matte painting *(noun)*
A detailed painting used in movies as background scenery. The large government warehouse at the end of *Raiders of the Lost Ark* and the Statute of Liberty in *Planet of the Apes* were really matte paintings.
3D models are now used instead of MATTE PAINTINGS.

Matt Foley *(proper noun)*
A motivational speaker on *Saturday Night Live* played by Chris Farley, who's "livin' in a van down by the river!"
The substitute teacher was so crazy and sweaty he was going all MATT FOLEY on us.

MCP *(proper noun)*
Short for Master Control Program. The evil artificial intelligence in the movie *Tron* that ruled over programs with an iron fist and attempted to take control over other computers and companies in the real world.
MCP is weak sauce compared to SKYnet.

Meatwad *(proper noun)*
The main character of *Aqua Team Hunger Force.* A childlike ball of meat that can change into many different objects, such as Samurai Abraham Lincoln and an igloo.
Tip for MEATWAD: If you look like a ball of meat, it's a good thing to be able to transform into something else.

8

Mecca lecca hi, mecca hiney ho *(phrase)*
A magic phrase spoken on *Pee-wee's Playhouse.*
> *Paul Reubens probably wishes he could say MECCA LECCA HI MECCA HINEY HO and magically get his career back.*

GEEK FACT

The character Cowboy Curtis on *Pee-wee's Playhouse* was played by actor Laurence Fishburne. In the episode "The Cowboy and the Cowntess," Miss Yvonne asks Cowboy Curtis out on a date. Cowboy Curtis is very nervous, and Pee-wee decides to help him out by dressing up as a girl so Cowboy Curtis can role-play the date beforehand.

midi-chlorians *(noun)*
Introduced in *Star Wars, Episode I: The Phantom Menace*, microorganisms that flow through every living thing and are in communication with the Force.
> *When MIDI-CHLORIANS were introduced in* The Phantom Menace, *I knew that* Star Wars *had Nuked the Fridge.*

Milton *(proper noun)*
Cartoon shorts by Mike Judge that served as the inspiration for the movie *Office Space*, which included the character of Milton, played by Stephen Root, who believes that someone has his stapler.
> *"Now, MILTON, don't be greedy. Let's pass it along and make sure everyone gets a piece."* —Office Space

model sheet *(noun)*
Used by animators, it is a sheet of drawings of a character in different positions and poses, used as a reference.
> *My MODEL SHEET would include me in all of my various positions, including my seventeen different ways of sitting on a couch.*

moment of Zen *(noun)*
1. A moment where one achieves the state of no-mind. 2. The last segment on *The Daily Show* that shows a funny video.
> *Ninjas often have a MOMENT OF ZEN while watching Jon Stewart.*

monolith *(noun)*

A device built by aliens that grants organisms wisdom. Responsible in *2001: A Space Odyssey* for helping prehistoric hominids discover tools and weapons, and an astronaut evolve into the Star Child. Its dimensions are 1×4×9 (the squares of the first three integers).

> *Don't understand the MONOLITH? Don't worry. No one else does either. It's kind of like most Pink Floyd songs—only people who are really high understand it—and then they no longer care.*

most atypical *(phrase)*

Amazing. From the movie *Bill and Ted's Excellent Adventure*.

> *No, that outfit does not make you look fat. It makes you look MOST ATYPICAL and bodacious.*

motion capture *(noun)*

"Mocap" for short. A technique in which someone is hooked up to sensors so that his or her body's movements are tracked, fed into a computer, and used to animate a digital character.

> *Actors have made a living being MOTION CAPTURE specialists, including Andy Serkis, who played Gollum in Peter Jackson's* Lord of the Rings.

moviegating *(noun)*

The art of following closely behind another vehicle to watch a movie playing on a television in the vehicle.

> *There are many activities that can prolong your life—exercise, eating healthy, regular visits to the doctor—but MOVIEGATING is not one of them.*

MST3K *(proper noun)*

Short for *Mystery Science Theater 3000*, a television show that featured a viewer and two robots watching and making fun of bad movies from the 1950s and '60s.

> MST3K *is one of the greatest comedy shows of all time.*

Necron-99 *(proper noun)*
A robot assassin in the 1977 Ralph Bakshi movie *Wizards*. He travelled the countryside killing fairies and little bunny wabbits. In the film, he is later "reprogrammed" by the good wizard Avatar and renamed Peace.
NECRON-99 was voiced by David Proval, who went on to play Richie Aprile on The Sopranos.

GEEK FACT

Fans have speculated that Necron-99 was an inspiration for the *Star Wars* character Boba Fett, who debuted in the much-derided made-for-TV 1978 *Star Wars Christmas Special*. Although even the most die-hard *Star Wars* fans are embarrassed by the *Star Wars Christmas Special*, the animated sequence with Boba Fett was actually pretty cool.

---

neutral zone *(noun)*
The area between two territories belonging to different powers. If entered, it was considered a hostile act. Seen in *Star Trek,* it usually caused conflict between some combination of the Federation, Klingons, and the Romulans.
In the original Star Trek *series, the Klingon NEUTRAL ZONE was also known as the Organian Neutral Zone, after the inhabitants of Organia IV, who established the area.*

Nosferatu *(proper noun)*
The original vampire from the 1929 German film of the same name. He is known for being bald, all white, and having pointy ears and long, sharp fingers.
NOSFERATU does not have much teen appeal.

nuking the fridge *(noun)*
A point in a movie that is so outrageous that it lessens the impact of subsequent scenes. The phrase supposedly originated on the Internet Movie Database message boards and was taken from the movie *Indiana Jones and the Crystal Skull* when Indiana escapes a nuclear blast by enclosing himself in a fridge that is hurled for miles, after which Indie gets out without a scratch.
NUKE THE FRIDGE is to movies what jump the shark is to TV shows.

Number 6 *(proper noun)*
The main character in the British TV show *The Prisoner* played by Patrick "Longshanks" McGoohan. Number 6 was trapped in The Village for unknown reasons, most likely a secret he knows, and prevented from escaping by Rovers, or large balloons.
The actor who played NUMBER 6 later went on to play Edward I in the movie Braveheart.

OCD *(noun)*
Short for obsessive Cullen disorder. Referring to Edward Cullen of the movie *Twilight*.
OCD? Cullen? OMG. LOL. LMAO. Please. Team Jacob all the way. He's hot!

OME *(phrase)*
Oh my, Edward!
OME, it's Robert Pattinson! I didn't know he was also in Harry Potter!

GEEK QUIZ

Which comedic television actor developed the technique of filming TV comedies before a live audience, which is still in use today?

a. Steve Allen

b. Dick Van Dyke

c. Desi Arnaz

d. Alfred Hitchcock

Answer: c

Padawan *(proper noun)*
A Jedi apprentice serving under a Jedi knight.
Knick-knack PADAWAN, give the bantha a bone. This ol' Tusken Raider went howling home.

GEEK FACT

Much like the knightly orders of the Middle Ages, there are many ranks among the Jedi. The youngest children are Initiates, or "Younglings." The next rank above Initiate is the Padawan, or "Apprentice." After many years of training, a Padawan becomes a Jedi Knight, the rank of the overwhelming number of Jedi. Only the truly wise and powerful attain the rank of Jedi Master.

Paul Dini *(proper noun)*

An Emmy Award–winning American writer, most notable for being one of the primary creators of *Batman: The Animated Series*, as well as other DC Animated Universe shows like *Superman: The Animated Series*, *Batman Beyond*, *Justice League*, and the comic book *Jingle Belle*, about the adventures of Santa Claus's rebellious teenage daughter. He later joined the writing team of the ABC TV series *Lost*.

Besides being one of the most lauded writers in all of geekdom, PAUL DINI is also an amateur stage magician.

Pee-wee's Playhouse *(proper noun)*

A Saturday-morning kids show starring Paul Reubens's childlike alter ego Pee-wee Herman. During its run, the show received fifteen Emmy Awards and received rave critical reviews, including from kids show icon Bob Keeshan (better known as "Captain Kangaroo"), who wrote, "With the possible exception of the *Muppets*, you can't find such creativity anywhere on TV."

During the first season of PEE-WEE'S PLAYHOUSE, *the character of Captain Carl was played by Phil Hartman.*

phaser *(noun)*

A handheld energy weapon used in the *Star Trek* universe. Derived from the phrase "photon maser" because lasers were not commonly known at the time of the original series.

Set your PHASERS to fun!

plant *(noun)*

An employee of a company or studio who writes a positive review of a movie on a website while claiming to be an unbiased anonymous source.

Any pre-release-date positive review is a PLANT, a spy! Kill the plants! Give them no water! Let them rot!

plot crowbar *(noun)*
When something unrealistic happens in a movie for the sole purpose of moving the plot along.
> *Fast forward to the PLOT CROWBAR. I'm bored as hell with this flick!*

GEEK FACT

Examples of plot crowbars:
Debra Winger's character dies of cancer in *Terms of Endearment*.
Truman Capote writes *In Cold Blood* in the movie *Capote*.
Pretty much every third scene in *The Matrix*.

pon farr *(noun)*
From the *Star Trek* universe, it is the Vulcan term used to describe the biological state in which Vulcans must either mate or die.
> *PON FARR . . . mating every seven years, which would be a 100 percent increase for many Trekkies.*

popcorn flick *(noun)*
A movie that has little depth, almost no social or artistic meaning, but is loads of fun from beginning to end. Most tend to be action films and dominate the summer and holiday season release schedules.
> *Calling a movie a POPCORN FLICK isn't so much damning it with faint praise as it is praising it with faint damnation.*

President Frankenstein *(proper noun)*
The name of David Carradine's character in the Roger Corman film *Death Race 2000*, a film about a race whose goal was to run over as many people as possible.
> *In the remake of* Death Race, *the PRESIDENT FRANKENSTEIN character was played by Jason "The Transporter" Statham.*

GEEK FACT

Roger Corman is known for his cheap B-movies, but many famous filmmakers started their career with him including: Martin Scorcese, Francis Ford Coppolla, James Cameron, Jack Nicholson, and Robert DeNiro.

the prestige *(noun)*

Magic tricks have three steps: the pledge, the turn, and the prestige. The pledge is the magician's reveal of something ordinary, the turn is to make something ordinary extraordinary, and the prestige is the final effect. A movie was made based on the book by Christopher Priest, starring Christian Bale and Hugh Jackman, two illusionists at odds with each other.

THE PRESTIGE *of the movie was that it had an amazing ending.*

Prime Directive *(proper noun)*

In the *Star Trek* universe, the Prime Directive is Starfleet General Order 1, which forbids Starfleet personnel from interfering in the development of societies that have not yet achieved sufficient technology to achieve interstellar travel. The Prime Directive was first defined in the original *Star Trek* episode "Bread and Circuses" as: *No identification of self or mission. No interference with the social development of said planet. No references to space or the fact that there are other worlds or civilizations.*

"A star captain's most solemn oath is that he will give his life, even his entire crew, rather than violate the PRIME DIRECTIVE." — *Captain James T. Kirk, in the* Star Trek *episode "The Omega Glory"*

proof of concept *(noun)*

A presentation that proves that a project will work in the desired way. Used by filmmakers to prove they can accomplish a difficult task.

PROOF OF CONCEPT has been used by Pixar for their movies and by Robert Rodriguez for Sin City.

proton pack *(noun)*

In the film *Ghostbusters* (one of the greatest movies of all time), it is the primary weapon of the Ghostbusters. An unlicensed nuclear accelerator used to capture ghosts by firing a proton stream that polarizes negatively charged energy.

"Why worry? Each of us is wearing an unlicensed nuclear accelerator on his back." —Dr. Peter Venkman in Ghostbusters

GEEK FACT

The Ghostbusters' weapons are indeed proton packs in the script. But in the movie no one ever actually says the term "proton pack." Not once. The closest they come is when Venkman is tallying up the bill for the hotel manager after they catch their first ghost, and he charges him for "proton recharge."

Rabbit of Caerbannog *(proper noun)*
A deadly rabbit in Monty Python's *Quest for the Holy Grail* that kills many men before being killed by the Holy Hand Grenade of Antioch.
The RABBIT OF CAERBANNOG especially hates people who dislike British humor.

rage *(noun)*
A genetically engineered virus that causes an outbreak of running zombies in *28 Days Later.*
There is nothing worse than RAGE zombies.

GEEK FACT

Geekphosophy
Why are the genetically engineered "mistakes" in movies always bad? What about a genetically engineered virus that makes you just a little taller, smarter, and better looking?
Guess that wouldn't be a very compelling movie.

Raoul Duke *(proper noun)*
Hunter S. Thompson's alter ego, the main character in *Fear and Loathing in Las Vegas.* Played by Johnny Depp in the film.
Much like RAOUL DUKE, I also have an alternate identity when I go to Las Vegas.

Ray Harryhausen *(proper noun)*

A special effects master who specialized in using stop-motion to animate movie monsters. His credits include the original *Clash of the Titans*, *Mighty Joe Young*, *The 7th Voyage of Sinbad*, and *Jason and the Argonauts*.

RAY HARRYHAUSEN's Mighty Joe Young *is the only stop-motion animated tear jerker ever made.*

The Razzies *(proper noun)*

The Golden Raspberries. An award ceremony founded in 1981 with "worst of" categories such as "worst movie" and "worst actor."

Past RAZZIE winners include Halle Berry for Catwoman *and Tom Green for* Freddy Got Fingered. *They both showed up at the ceremony to accept their awards.*

red-band trailer *(noun)*

A movie trailer that displays a red rating card instead of a green one. It is not allowed for general audiences due to R-rated content such as profanity, nudity, and violence.

Every time I see a RED-BAND TRAILER, I cover my eyes.

red or blue pill *(phrase)*

Making the choice between the painful truth of enlightenment or comfortable ignorance. The same choice that Neo had to make in *The Matrix*.

You know, if Morpheus were smart he would not have offered Neo the RED OR BLUE PILL. He'd have been much smarter to offer the red cherry or blue suppository.

Red Dwarf *(proper noun)*

A comedic science-fiction TV series from Great Britain that aired on the BBC from 1988 to 1999.

RED DWARF . . . only on the BBC could you name the hero Ace Rimmer and get away with it.

red shirt *(noun)*

Stock member of a *Star Trek* starship. Members of security, they wore a red shirt and always seemed to be the first to die.

Do you mind changing into this RED SHIRT?

replicant *(noun)*
A bioengineered artificial human in *Blade Runner*.
> *In order to determine whether an individual is a REPLICANT or a human, the Voight-Kampff machine is used to test his or her emotional responses to stimuli.*

GEEK FACT
Geek Note
Voight-Kampff is not to be confused with *Mein Kampf*.

Robby the Robot *(proper noun)*
A very tall robot that was in the 1956 movie *Forbidden Planet* and has since become a sci-fi icon and appeared in the *Twilight Zone*, *The Phantom Menace*, *Futurama*, and *The Addams Family*.
> *ROBBY THE ROBOT was designed by Robert Kinoshita, who also designed Robot B-9 for the TV show* Lost in Space.

Rolo Tomasi *(proper noun)*
A name created by Ed Exley for the killer of his father in the fantastic 1997 film *L.A. Confidential*. The police never caught the man who killed Exley's father, so he invented a name for the murderer: Rolo Tomasi. Later in the movie, using the name helps Exley identify the traitor within the police force.
> *ROLO TOMASI was created exclusively for the movie and did not appear in the novel.*

rom com *(noun)*
The hip way to say "romantic comedy."
> *Come on, honey. A ROM COM again?*

rotoscope *(noun)*
A technique in animation where live-action film frames are traced over frame by frame for 2D animation.
> *Disney used the ROTOSCOPE technique in many of its early films. So did Ralph Bakshi for his version of* The Lord of the Rings, *although some of the scenes looks like he might have been doing it with his eyes closed.*

The Schwartz *(proper noun)*
A powerful force in the universe, as explained by Yogurt in *Spaceballs*. A parody of the Force from the *Star Wars* films.
> *May THE SCHWARTZ be with you!*

serial *(noun)*
Serialized films popular from the silent era to the '50s that were adventurous in nature, much like the pulp fiction of the time, and usually ended in a cliffhanger. Served as an inspiration for both the *Indiana Jones* and *Star Wars* films.
> *You know the best way to watch a SERIAL? With milk. HAHAHA. LOL. LMAO!!!*

shark-repellent bat spray *(noun)*
An over-the-top utility belt item in the 1966 *Batman* movie. It is used to deter a rubber shark attacking Batman while he is hanging onto a helicopter ladder.
> *You take the SHARK-REPELLENT BAT SPRAY. I'll take the Batwing.*

shot for shot *(noun)*
A technique in filming a comic book adaptation where scenes from the comic book are recreated shot for shot, sometimes ditching a storyboard altogether and using the comic as a guide.
> *Examples of SHOT FOR SHOT remakes:* Sin City *and* 300.

show runner *(noun)*
A person who is responsible for the day-to-day operations of a television show. Did you know that the show runners for *The Simpsons* in its first two seasons were Matt Groening, James L. Brooks, and Sam Simon? No wonder it became a classic.

What do you call a SHOW RUNNER who doesn't make it to work? A "No Show!"

Skynet *(proper noun)*
The super-sophisticated computer system in *The Terminator* films, created by Cyberdyne Systems, that is responsible for creating the sentient robots that try to exterminate humanity.

Other things created by SKYNET: The Clapper and the hovering hula hoop. Just stand there as it goes around you . . . no movement necessary.

GEEK QUIZ

Sometimes movie titles, once translated into other languages, become unintentionally hilarious in the original language. Which of the following is *not* a movie title as it has been translated to another language?

a. *The Young People Who Traverse Dimensions While Wearing Sunglasses (The Matrix)*, France

b. *One Night, Big Belly (Knocked Up)*, China

c. *Captain Supermarket (Army of Darkness)*, Japan

d. *Multiply the Children, One by One (Cheaper by the Dozen)*, Germany

Answer: d

---

sleeper hit *(noun)*
Any form of entertainment that is unexpectedly successful.

Some sensational SLEEPER HIT smashes are There's Something about Mary, The Shawshank Redemption, *and* Shark Tale.

slimed (verb)

To have green goo thrown over one's head on the Nickelodeon show *You Can't Do That on Television*. Also, in the movie *Ghostbusters*, to be covered in ectoplasmic goo after a too-close encounter with a ghost.

"He SLIMED me." —Dr. Peter Venkman in Ghostbusters

Smurf (proper noun)

Besides being the name of the little blue characters on the *Smurfs* cartoon, the word "smurf" can mean almost anything, such as "to be" or "to make."

SMURF you, you smurfing smurf smurfer.

Space Jockey (proper noun)

In the 1979 movie *Alien*, a fossilized extraterrestrial seen sitting in the pilot's seat of a derelict spaceship. The Space Jockey was obviously the victim of a Xenomorph.

My brother Joel got crusty and dirty from playing World of Warcraft *so long that now he looks like the SPACE JOCKEY.*

space opera (noun)

A genre of science fiction that emphasizes the dramatic elements and major sci-fi tropes and downplays the scientific elements.

Star Wars *is the most famous SPACE OPERA because of its epic scale and story involving starships, melodrama, and heroes and villains.*

spaghetti western (noun)

Italian-produced westerns made with a mostly Italian cast and crew and typified by low budgets. They often dealt with issues involving Mexico and the United States. Examples are *Savage Guns*, *Navajo Joe*, *A Fistful of Dollars*, *Django*, and *The Good, the Bad, and the Ugly*, considered by many to be one of the greatest films ever made—and rightly so!

Most SPAGHETTI WESTERNS were made by Italians, but most were shot in Spain.

spatial anomaly (noun)

A term commonly used in the *Star Trek* universe to describe any number of things, from a wormhole to an intelligent quasar bent on testing the intelligence or morality of the ship's crew.

I once found a SPATIAL ANOMALY in a pile of trash in my closet. It was a peace-seeking A.I., but I had to destroy it for the greater good, to clean my room.

Spider-Pig *(proper noun)*
The name for Plopper, a pig in *The Simpsons Movie*.
   SPIDER-PIG, Spider-Pig, does whatever a Spider-Pig does.

Spirited Away *(proper noun)*
A Japanese animated film by Hayao Miyazaki about a girl who works at a bathhouse for spirits. Won the Oscar for Best Animated Feature and has made more money than any other film in Japan.
   SPIRITED AWAY is a tale that combines the Japanese love of bathhouses with their love of spirits.

The Spirit of Christmas *(proper noun)*
A precursor to *South Park*, made by Trey Parker and Matt Stone in 1995, which featured the cast of *South Park* and a fight between Jesus and Santa. It spread quickly after a limited number of friends were given the video as a gift.
   First saw THE SPIRIT OF CHRISTMAS in a goth club in 1995.

spoiler alert *(noun)*
A warning to readers of a review that there will be information that may ruin the surprises in a film, TV show, or comic book. If necessary, always use a spoiler alert.
   SPOILER ALERT: Everyone dies at the end of this book.

Starscream *(proper noun)*
A screeching Decepticon Jet that was second in command to Megatron and known for treacherous behavior in the *Transformers* cartoon. He was attempting to gain Megatron's leadership position when he was killed. He was later reborn as a "spark."
   Both STARSCREAM and Cobra Commander in the G.I. Joe cartoon were voiced by Chris Latta.

Steamboy *(proper noun)*
The most expensive Japanese animated movie ever. Set in the steampunk genre, it is about a boy who has a knack for building Victorian era-inspired mechanical devices, such as a flying machine that runs on steam.
   There is also a Korean movie called STEAMBOY that follows one young boy's dream to open his very own dry cleaners.

Stephen Colbert *(proper noun)*
Host of Comedy Central's *The Colbert Report* and arguably one of the most successful geeks in pop culture. Besides being an avid player of D&D as a young geek, he can still recite Aragorn's lineage for at least four generations.

> *Kids have Dora and Boots. Their parents have Jon Stewart and STEPHEN COLBERT.*

stop motion *(noun)*
A type of animation used in claymation or Ray Harryhausen films where a miniature is filmed frame by frame with incremental movements. In the final film the miniature appears to move on its own.

> *STOP-MOTION characters have been giving me nightmares for years: talking ventriloquist dolls, giant monsters from Sinbad movies, and Gumby.*

stormtrooper effect *(noun)*
Derived from *Star Wars* and coined by Roger Ebert, this is the phenomenon in movies where, despite all logic, enemy fighters are unable to hit the outnumbered heroes.

> *Without the STORMTROOPER EFFECT, movies would be about five minutes long and end with the hero dying.*

Strike Team *(proper noun)*
The tactical antigang police unit led by Vic Mackey in the television show *The Shield*. To achieve their goals, they used illegal methods such as robbing gangs and giving protection to gang members.

> *When there is something strange in the neighborhood, who you gonna call? The STRIKE TEAM!*

Stripperella *(proper noun)*
A cartoon created by Stan Lee about a secret agent who is also a stripper, voiced by Pamela Anderson.

> *The plot of STRIPPERELLA differs from the classical tale of Cinderella in that instead of Prince Charming there's Prince Old Sweaty Guy with Lots of Cash.*

suicide booth *(noun)*

A machine that assists the user in committing suicide. Forms of this machine have appeared in many works of fiction, including *Star Trek* and *Futurama*.

> *In* Futurama, *the SUICIDE BOOTH resembles a phone booth and costs one quarter per use.*

Super Friends *(proper noun)*

A cartoon in the 1970s and 1980s based on the Justice League of America. It starred Batman, Superman, and Wonder Woman, among others, and even Wonder Dog.

> *Best part of* SUPER FRIENDS*? "Wonder Twin powers . . . activate! Form of . . . a bucket of water!"*

GEEK FACT

The narrator of *Super Friends* was none other than Ted Knight from *Caddyshack* and *The Mary Tyler Moore Show.*

Sword of Omens *(proper noun)*

The name of Lion-O's sword on *Thundercats* that gives him "sight beyond sight."

> *If I could choose between the SWORD OF OMENS and He-Man's power sword, I would choose the power sword because it appears to give you a tan and cool red underpants.*

tachyon particles *(noun)*

Subatomic particles in the *Star Trek* universe that usually can be used to solve any problem in a display of deus ex machina.

> *I tried to reconfigure the main sensor array to emit a constant stream of TACHYON PARTICLES to save my last relationship. Didn't work.*

Takashi Miike *(proper noun)*

A filmmaker from Japan who creates twisted and controversial films. *Ichi the Killer* and *Audition* are shocking and yet high quality.

> *TAKASHI MIIKE'S favorite movie is* Starship Troopers.

TARDIS *(proper noun)*

Short for Time and Relative Dimension in Space. A time machine used by Doctor Who and created by the Time Lords in the shape of a 1950s British police box.

> *I need to take a TARDIS and travel to an alternate universe where* Doctor Who *is on TV all day, every day!*

Ted McGinley curse *(noun)*

Named for the patron saint of jumping the shark, actor Ted McGinley. According to the curse, any time Ted McGinley is added to the cast of a TV show, it is doomed for cancellation.

> *Behold, the power of the TED MCGINLEY CURSE! Is there any way we could get McGinley on* American Idol *and* Survivor?

GEEK FACT

Being geeks of science, let us consider the evidence for the Ted McGinley curse:

- *Happy Days.* One of the most successful sitcoms of the late '70s. McGinley joins the cast in the early '80s, and the show is soon cancelled.
- *The Love Boat.* Ditto.
- *Sports Night.* The critically acclaimed show (the one Aaron Sorkin did before *The West Wing*). McGinley joins, and the show is soon cancelled. Perhaps Sorkin learned his lesson, because McGinley only appeared in three episodes of *The West Wing*.

---

test screening *(noun)*

A preliminary screening held by producers for a special audience to test a movie and get feedback so that changes can be made before wide release.

> *I once went to a TEST SCREENING for a movie called* The Haunting. *Before my valuable input, the ending was completely different.*

theremin *(noun)*

An electronic musical device that creates the eerie siren sound used in 1950s sci-fi movies. The THEREMIN was used in *The Day the Earth Stood Still*, *The She Creature*, and *Queen of Blood*.

> *Hey, someone turn down the friggin' THEREMIN. It's creeping me out!*

Thundarr the Barbarian *(proper noun)*

A Saturday morning cartoon of the early '80s, chronicling the adventures of Thundarr the Barbarian and his companions Princess Airel (a sorceress) and Ookla the Mok (an obvious rip-off of Chewbacca). It contained tropes of both fantasy and science fiction.

"He is . . . THUNDARR THE BARBARIAN*!"*

GEEK FACT

"Ookla" was supposedly taken from how UCLA (University of California, Los Angeles) is pronounced.

GEEK QUIZ

Fictional spacecraft are as big a part of sci-fi as fictional alien races. Every geek should know his starships. What is the name of the spacecraft in the movie *Alien* that is towing mineral ore from Thedus to Earth?

a. *Alexei Leonov*

b. *Nostromo*

c. *Nemesis*

d. *The Schwanschtüppen*

Answer: b

Thundercats *(proper noun)*

A cartoon in the 1980s about a group of anthropomorphic cats and their battle against Mumm-Ra and the mutants of Plun-Darr. Like other '80s cartoons, there was also an awesome toy line, which led to great times for American children.

The voice actor for Lion-O, leader of the THUNDERCATS, *was Larry Kenney, who has also voiced Count Chocula and Sonny the Cuckoo Bird.*

torture porn *(noun)*

The term to describe horror movies where the characters are subject to horrible and over-the-top torture solely for the entertainment of the viewing audience. Examples are *Hostel*, *Saw*, *Wolf Creek*, and *The Devil's Rejects*.

When a girl comes over, Drew always hides his TORTURE PORN collection.

Transformers *(proper noun)*

A cartoon, comic, toy line, and movie series about a group of "robots in disguise" from the planet Cybertron who can transform into vehicles such as a cars, jets, and trucks with flame-designs. The Autobots are the good Transformers, lead by Optimus Prime, that fight against the Decepticons, the evil Transformers, lead by Megatron.

The first TRANSFORMERS movie was a cartoon, and was world-shattering in a child's eye because many of the original Transformers were killed.

Trek band *(noun)*

Star Trek-themed bands such as Klingon heavy metal bands.

Some of the best TREK BANDS include Earth, Solar Wind, and Fire, The Stone Temple Space Pilots, and the Insane Klingon Posse.

Trekker *(noun)*

Pretty much the same thing as a Trekkie, only Trekkers want to be taken more seriously. Good luck with that.

TREKKER, Trekkie . . . what's the difference?

Trekkie *(noun)*

A fan devoted to all things *Star Trek*.

Famous TREKKIES include Seinfeld's *Jason Alexander,* Frasier's *Kelsey Grammer, and actor/comedian Ben Stiller.*

Treknobabble *(noun)*

The scientific explanations in the *Star Trek* universe that are not necessarily completely scientific but seem plausible enough to move the plot forward.

Supposedly on Star Trek: The Next Generation, *when the story needed some science, the script would have a note written as <tech> where TREKNOBABBLE would be inserted at a later time.*

> ## GEEK FACT
>
> The *Star Trek* universe includes alcoholic beverages such as Tranya, which appeared in the original series. Romulan Ale was given to Kirk by Bones in The *Wrath of Khan*. Once you take a sip of Romulan Ale, you become instantly drunk, maybe that's why it is illegal.

tribble *(noun)*
From a famous *Star Trek* episode, "The Trouble with Tribbles." Cute, tiny, and furry aliens that reproduce very quickly in high volumes and soon overwhelm the ship.
   TRIBBLES are more viral than cat videos on the Internet.

Triumph *(proper noun)*
The insult comic dog, played by Robert Smigel, that often appeared on *Late Night with Conan O'Brien* and insulted *Star Wars* fans waiting in line for *Star Wars Episode II: Attack of the Clones.*
   TRIUMPH is the funniest talking dog ever.

Tru Blood *(proper noun)*
From the HBO Series *True Blood*, it is synthetic bottled blood sold legally for vampires as an alternative to real blood, which led to vampires coming out into the public eye.
   TRU BLOOD's slogan is, "Friends don't let friends drink friends."

GEEK QUIZ

What is the name of the rival town to Springfield on the TV show *The Simpsons*, which included a dispute over the location of a lemon tree?

a. Shelbyville

b. Ogdenville

c. North Haverbrook

d. Butano Gardens

Answer: a

---

twiguy *(noun)*
A male obsessed with *Twilight*.
> *"One dark and cold night, my wife made me watch* Twilight. *Since then I have never been the same. I became a TWIGUY. Jacob!"*

twihard *(noun)*
A *Twilight* fan.
> *I used to make fun of* Twilight *until I saw it. I am more than a TWI-HARD now.*

twist ending *(noun)*
A secret reveal at the end that changes how the story is perceived—used often in literature and M. Night Shyamalan movies.
> *The best TWIST ENDINGS were in* The Sixth Sense, The Usual Suspects, *and* The Ten Commandments. *The Red Sea parting? Who would have seen that coming?*

Unicron *(proper noun)*
A giant Transformer planet that is the main antagonist in the *Transformers Movie* from the 1980s.
> *UNICRON is now just a floating horned head in outer space. Awkward!*

Uwe Boll *(proper noun)*
Generally regarded negatively as a director of such crappy video game adaptations as *Alone in the Dark* and *Bloodrayne*.
> *UWE BOLL supposedly uses German investors for his films, who get tax write-offs for their investments, which would be offset if the movie makes money. So they are better off making a box office bomb à la* The Producers. *Now it all makes sense.*

verisimilitude *(noun)*
A measure of the realism or "truthiness" of a movie or other art form.
> The Transformers *films are lacking in VERISIMILITUDE.*

Vulcan mind meld *(noun)*
In the *Star Trek* universe, a Vulcan technique involving physical contact where thoughts and experiences can be shared between two individuals.
> *I met this hot chick at a* Star Trek *Convention and later we had a total VULCAN MIND MELD!*

walk-off *(noun)*

A street-level modeling competition in the movie *Zoolander*, where two models compete with each other in walking the runway.

Welcome to the dark underbelly of the modeling world: a WALK-OFF judged by David Bowie.

GEEK QUIZ

What is *not* a blooper that was in the original *Star Wars* movie and caught by fans?

a. Darth Vader's chest plate is on backwards when he is fighting Obi-Wan Kenobi.

b. A stormtrooper hits his head on the top of a door frame when he is entering the control room.

c. On the Jawa's transport vehicle, an eye is visible through an eye hole in R2-D2.

d. In the *Millennium Falcon*, a soda can is seen on the floor in the hallway.

Answer: d

---

wampa *(noun)*

The creature in *The Empire Strikes Back* that resembles the abominable snowman and takes Luke Skywalker hostage before having his arm cut off by a light saber.

Beware of WAMPA.

Wilhelm scream *(noun)*

A stock sound effect of a man screaming that has been used in over 200 films since 1951. Credits include *Star Wars*, *Raiders of the Lost Ark*, and *The Lord of the Rings*.

Whoever is behind this WILHELM SCREAM needs a Xanax.

The Wire *(proper noun)*
A famed HBO television series set in Baltimore, Maryland, that was created, produced, and primarily written by former police reporter David Simon. While it won critical acclaim, it never gained as much popularity as *The Sopranos* during its five seasons.

Lessons learned from THE WIRE *include: you cannot do more with less; in a bureaucracy, those who put their careers ahead of their jobs will advance, those who don't will not; and collaboration is usually more profitable than fighting.*

wire fu *(noun)*
Hong Kong action films where the actors who are fighting are obviously floating around on wires.

WIRE FU uses wires? Wait a minute. You mean Chinese people can't fly?

GEEK QUIZ

The Emperor was a mysterious Jedi Master in the original *Star Wars* movies and was revealed to be Palpatine in the prequel movies. But did he have yet another title? What is the Sith title of Emperor Palpatine?

a. Darth Sidious

b. Darth Maul

c. Darth Tyranus

d. Darth Malak

Answer: a

---

worst ever *(phrase)*
From the Comic Book Guy in *The Simpsons*, the phrase "Worst _____ ever" can be used to describe any number of horrible things.

That was the WORST date with Jessica Alba EVER.

Xenomorph *(noun)*
An extraterrestrial creature featured in the *Alien* movies. Its blood is strongly acidic and it has an extra protruding mouth.

XENOMORPH is from the Greek, meaning "strange shape."

Z movie *(noun)*

A movie of such low quality that it falls below even a B or C movie. Examples include *Plan 9 from Outer Space* and *Manos: The Hands of Fate*.

If you really just want to make out, take your chick to a Z MOVIE.

zoom, enhance *(verb)*

Commonly seen in television and movies where a blurry image is sharpened to the point where an important clue is found.

Wait, focus on sector A5. ZOOM, ENHANCE. My God! 'Twas Professor Plum in the library.

CONCLUSION

Well, we have given you, faithful reader, a lot of geek data and lore to ponder and absorb. We hope you non-geeks and wannabe geeks also have gained a good introduction to our nomenclature and activities. But there are many other things in the world to geek out on. We encourage you to continue your explorations of the things you love including not only comic books, movies, and video games, but also such activities as LARPing and writing fanfiction. But whatever you do, do it with typical geek passion and gusto.

As more and more people are captivated by technology and formerly exclusively geek genres such as science fiction, fantasy, and superheroes become mainsream, we see that geeks are taking over the world . . . but not in some evil Lex Luthor way. So, put on your *Star Wars* Imperial Stormtrooper helmet, turn on your *Lord of the Rings* filk music, and geek out to your heart's content. May the geek be with you!

ABOUT THE
AUTHORS

Gregory Bergman is the author of the *WTF?* humor series including *WTF? How to Survive 101 of Life's Worst F*#!-ing Situations, WTF? College, WTF? Work* and *WTF? Women.* He is also the author of four additional books: *101 Things You–and John McCain—Didn't Know about Sarah Palin; Bizzwords; –Isms;* and *The Little Book of Bathroom Philosophy.* Mr. Bergman also performs stand-up comedy regularly in his hometown of Los Angeles. His act mostly consists of poking fun at his own geeky tendencies, such as his need to sleep with a light saber for protection.

Josh Lambert has been and always shall be a geek. He received degrees from UC Berkeley and USC. He owns a vast comic book collection, engages in computer animation and illustration, and makes his living valuing going concerns using financial models. Josh currently lives in Sacramento, CA and roams the city at night as a crime-fighting ninja. Things that make Josh geek out: Gamer Girls, Alan Moore comics, and *The Simpsons.*